TALES
FROM THE
CREWROOM

TALES
FROM THE
CREWROOM

David Berry

with cartoons by 'HOLLY'

OSPREY
AEROSPACE

First Published in 1990 by Osprey Publishing
Limited
59 Grosvenor Street
London W1X 9DA

British Library Cataloguing in Publication Data
Berry, David
    Tales from the crewroom.
    1. Great Britain. Royal Air Force—Biographies
    I. Title
    358.40092
ISBN 0-85045-977-X

Editor Dennis Baldry

Printed by
Guernsey Press,
Channel Islands,
United Kingdom

CONTENTS

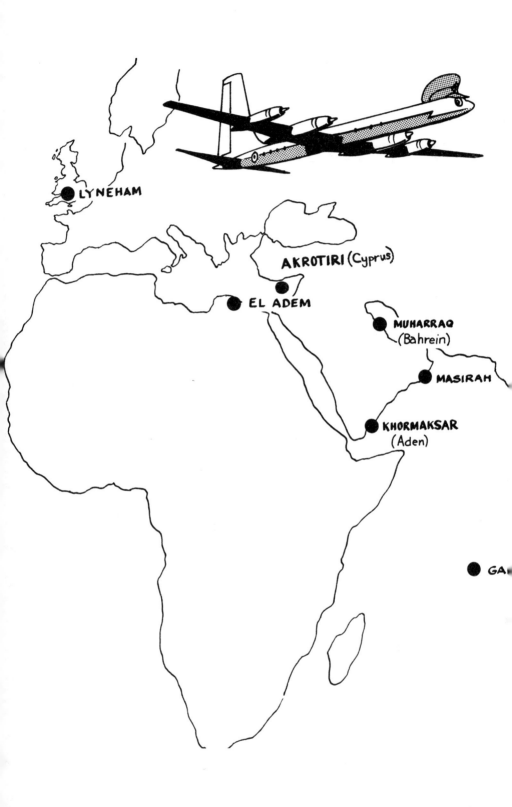

LYNEHAM

AKROTIRI (Cyprus)

EL ADEM

MUHARRAQ
(Bahrein)

MASIRAH

KHORMAKSAR
(Aden)

GA

CHANGI
(Singapore)

FOREWORD

THERE IS A TENDENCY TO THINK OF FOLKLORE AS A THING OF
THE DISTANT PAST, BUT EVERY AGE AND WALK OF LIFE HAS ITS
LEGENDS AND SOME TIMES AND PLACES ARE MORE FERTILE FOR
THESE TO BE SOWN AND CULTIVATED...

... The flying crewroom must be a rich pasture in this respect. Folklore
is created by there being a story to tell, one worthy of telling and an
audience eager to listen. But the pattern of folklore is not complete
without that story being taken up by one of the listeners and related to
another audience. Naturally, in the process, some simplification for ease
of telling might take place, perhaps accompanied by exaggeration for
effect—and a folk tale is born.

Thus this book which will seek to amuse and entertain by re-telling
some of the 'Tales from the Crewroom'—unexaggerated, of course!

I dedicate it to my wife, Valerie, who was at home, raising four children
and training to be a teacher whilst I travelled the world 'gathering
material'!

1
The Changi Slip

The springboard for these stories is the period of the 1960s and early 70s, when the size of the Royal Air Force transport aircraft fleet was at its height—a time when we had left behind the trauma of the Second World War but still felt a duty in global defence matters. To support this we had a new generation of up-to-date long range transport aircraft—Britannias, Comets, Belfasts and VC10s. In the short range world were the Argosys, Andovers and Beverleys. In the latter part of the period, along came the Hercules which, with the surviving VC10s, were to inherit the mantle of transport flying when all the others were long gone. For, in 1975, came the big axe, defence cuts annihilating this wonderful fleet of Royal Air Force transport aircraft and the life that went with them. It was sad to see a force with such spirit killed off.

Transport Command's major job was to keep our overseas garrisons regularly supplied, whilst being ready to support UK forces in trouble spots around the world, and exercising with military units to ensure that we could fulfil this latter role. But our primary task did tend to overshadow all the others. Our main bases were located in the Mediterranean, the Middle and Far East. So our supply chain was set up through all these areas and we carried servicemen and their families and all manner of supplies. This route became known as the 'Changi Slip'.

The meaning of the word 'slip' should be expanded upon for the uninitiated. With the introduction of the Britannia and the requirement to fly overseas most of the men and their families, equipment and stores, maximum utilization of this sophisticated aircraft was very important. The plan, therefore, was that aircraft should keep moving. At each staging post it was refuelled and at every other staging post a fresh crew took the aircraft on its next leg. Thus the crew that had been flying it 'slipped' ...

and slept before waiting for the next aircraft in the pattern. This meant that the aircraft took about 30 hours to fly from the UK to Singapore. It would spend 12 or so hours there being off-loaded and reloaded before starting its return journey. So the aircraft was out and back within three days. But the crew's absence was considerably longer. The shortest planned time would be about ten days, but because of inevitable delays this could easily extend to a fortnight or three weeks—but the sun shone, the *Keo*, *Amstel* and *Tiger* flowed—and stories were told . . .

EL ADEM

KHORMAKSAR 'LOCAL'

GAN

CYPRUS

CHANGI YOU ARE HERE

BAHREIN

MASIRAH- 'OIL DRUM CITY'

At the beginning of each month a detailed plan was produced, outlining how crews would be utilized in order to keep the aircraft moving. Dreamers! On 'Day One' this plan would turn to worms. All that was needed was for one aircraft to go unserviceable and the whole thing had to be adjusted. This provided crews on the 'slip' with a major pastime—working out how they would fare in the changed plan. This could be the cause of some acrimony, for a golden rule was 'first in, first out'. This, on the surface, seems quite fair in that the crew that had been longest at a particular staging post were top of the list to leave. But it was not as

simple as that. Circumstances could occur where 'overtaking' took place—and then the feathers would fly!

Changes in world affairs dictated that the route to Singapore be altered over the years. The earliest route started with Lyneham to El Adem, near Tobruk in North Africa. This was a God-forsaken hole, only out-classed by the next stop, RAF Khormaksar, Aden. These two stops and the location of the Singapore Island base changed over the years, but the constant element was the staging post on the island of Gan, part of the chain of Maldive Islands in the Indian Ocean. Next stop Singapore, at RAF Changi, close to the gaol made notorious by the Japanese during World War 2.

There we ha\ e the earliest route—Lyneham, El Adem, Khormaksar, Gan, Changi. This changed in time with the Britannias being relocated in the UK at RAF Brize Norton. RAF Akrotiri, Cyprus replaced El Adem; the next stop became RAF Muharraq in the Persian Gulf and later still RAF Masirah, further East. Gan remained faithful throughout and towards the end of the era RAF Tengah was used in Singapore.

Here is the web for some of the stories that will follow—stories of the 'Changi Slip', an operating plan aimed at maximum and efficient aircraft utilization.

It had not always been so. In previous times, dominated by the Hastings aircraft, things were not done at such a pace. A crew would stay with its aircraft, hopping stage by stage to the destination.

Many a tale is told of that different era when, because of poor communications and a lack of necessity, crews were much more autonomous. One such story is that of a Hastings on a trip to Australia, one destined, because of the distance and the number of night stops, to be a long trip. Destiny in this type of flying also includes the inevitable aircraft unserviceablity, and this aircraft had its share.

They eventually made it to Australia, where the Captain was approached by a young lady, to see if it would be possible to be taken back to the UK as an indulgence (spare seat) passenger. As she was a member of the RAAF, with her papers all in order, it was agreed—and off they set.

But then the 'Gremlins' struck. On the way home the aircraft was constantly unserviceable. At one point the delay was so protracted that the crew took part-time jobs! As the UK was eventually neared, but still only slowly, the Australian lady presents the Captain with a problem, '*I'm pregnant, and if we don't get to the UK soon, I'll be having the baby in this dump!*' Our gallant Captain is somewhat taken aback by this revelation and remonstrates with the young woman, telling her that, had he known she was 'in the family way', he would never have brought her from Australia. '*I wasn't pregnant when we left!*' she retorted!

2
Our Base in Darkest Wiltshire

Royal Air Force Lyneham, which lies between Swindon and Chippenham in North Wiltshire, was the original home of the RAF Britannias. Lyneham was a strange place—an illustration of how things happen by circumstance and with the benefit of hindsight ... It was never big enough for the job. It inherited its transport role from World War 2 days and was the main base for the first post-war purpose built transport aircraft, the Hastings. With these, the Royal Air Force established its long range transport flying strategy which was greatly expanded with the introduction, in 1959, of the Bristol Aircraft Britannia, a four-engined turboprop aircraft well to the fore in aviation development. The natural home for it was RAF Lyneham. But Lyneham, as it had been, could not cope and there began the building and alterations which went on and on. Thus the often made remark, '*Lyneham will be great—when it's finished!*'

This true story—and I repeat true, because I was there—is set at RAF Lyneham in the 1960s. As well as being the home of the Royal Air Force's Strategic Transport Force, the Comets and the Britannias, it was also the location for a Maintenance Unit specialising in the major overhaul of aircraft and their storage, if necessary.

Commanding the Unit was a Wing Commander of the Technical Branch. It so happened that this Wing Commander, in his earlier years, had participated in a scheme to give young Technical Officers a wider appreciation of their engineering role by allowing them to undergo pilot training. That is all they did—the training—before returning to their normal duties. It will transpire that this is of some significance to this story.

On a sunny day at RAF Lyneham, across at the Maintenance Unit, an English Electric Lightning required engine tests. This incredible aircraft can best be described as two enormous jet engines strapped together, one on top of the other, with the pilot perched on top, the whole being surrounded by aluminium—a potent piece of machinery. The aircraft was positioned for this test at the end of a disused runway. The canopy was not fitted, neither was the ejector seat. A wooden box was provided for the person who was to run the engines.

For some reason that has disappeared into the mists of time, the CO, the aforementioned Wing Commander, decided that he personally would carry out these engine runs. Head down, seated on the wooden box, he started the engines and began the test routine. High power settings were called for as the test progressed.

As full power was applied, the aircraft leaned forward, straining against the brakes and the wheel chocks. Suddenly, with a bang and a roar, the Lightning leapt over the chocks and went streaking down the runway!

The Wing Commander, in the few seconds as he hurtled along towards certain death, experienced an immediate recall of how to fly an aeroplane—and pulled back on the control column. Now he was airborne—alive—but with what could only be a deferred termination problem. He needed to remember all he could of his flying days to keep the Lightning airborne and, more to the point, to land it in one piece. And all this, only equipped with his long past very basic flying experience, in an aircraft of considerable weight, performance and complexity with the 'pilot' sitting on a wooden box with no flying helmet or canopy!

A full emergency was obviously declared—and the spectators turned out! But there was little anyone could do except keep the airfield clear and wait. There was some initial relief as it became clear that the CO did have the aircraft under some reasonable control as he circled Lyneham.

Such relief returned to anxiety as he made his first tentative approach to the runway. He was much too high and fast. Now the fear was that, on his next attempt, he would go to the other extreme and be too low and slow—a not unfounded apprehension; but the Wing Commander had the good sense to abandon this approach early and overshoot. Time was now a factor, as the aircraft had only a small amount of fuel at the start of the engine runs (probably a contribution towards its chock leaping act) so now, with the circling of the airfield and the two approaches, his fuel state was critical.

The Lightning once again started an approach to the runway. It was apparent that this was probably the last possible attempt by the increase in the unsteadiness of the flight, conveying to the onlookers the even more heightened anxiety of the 'pilot'. However, in spite of the approach resembling a weaving roller coaster, the Lightning arrived on the end of the runway and landed hard, but safely!

Such a story should have a happy ending but I believe that the Wing Commander was praised and admonished simultaneously and was probably of a somewhat nervous disposition from that day on!

Folk-lore lives on in the right environment, such as the Crew Room—but the tales are not necessarily about flying. Conversation will prompt a reminiscence. This tale would arise out of talk of parades, inspections and the like.

It is not the true (!) tale of the scruffy airman, who, on parade, is challenged by the Station Commander about his appearance. 'Look at your shoes', barks the CO, 'are those the best you have?' 'No Sir', replies AC Bloggs, 'I've got a better pair in the Barrack Block.' 'Well why aren't you wearing them then?' 'Cos they're brown, Sir!'

My tale concerns the time when I was a young flying instructor at No 2 Flying Training School, RAF Syerston. One day I was summoned to the presence of the Station Commander to be told that I was to take charge of the Station Guard of Honour. It came as no surprise to me that the post

was vacant for the tale of my predecessor's performance, the previous day, had spread like wild-fire.

The Guard of Honour had been formed up, with Flight Lieutenant X in front, to pay respects to the Air Officer Commanding, one of the famous Atcherley twins. He arrived by air, the aircraft stopping in the precise place, right on time. The Air Marshal descended the steps.

The Guard Commander started putting his men through the traditional routine—'*Guard of Honour, Slope Arms*'—'*Present Arms*'. Then he made a fateful mistake! '*Order Arms*'.

For those of less mature years, denied the joys of Arms Drill with the .303 Enfield rifle, some explanation is required. A Guard started with their rifles at the 'Order', that is with the butt resting on the ground and held against their right legs. The next command was 'Slope Arms' when the rifle was moved to the left shoulder. The final part of the ceremony was the 'Present Arms' when, with much banging and a little foot juggle, the men 'presented' their rifles before them, a symbolic 'giving'. Having held this position for a few seconds the process was reversed—'Slope Arms'—'Order Arms'. Those were the positions and that was the essential order!

Return now to our doomed Flight Lieutenant. He, in a position of some disadvantage—facing forward, his back to the men, had given the command 'Order Arms' when the Guard was at the 'Present'! The 'rules', just outlined, do not allow for this!

Consider the plight of his men. Some remembered a basic tenet, from their training days: if you are given a wrong order then you 'stand fast'. Therefore these, possessed of good memory, stayed at the 'Present'. Others, perhaps of a more pragmatic nature, thought 'Well, what he really means is Slope Arms', and duly went to that position. The remainder, possibly with lesser imagination, thought that, as 'Order Arms' had been given, they would go to that position, which they did in a variety of ways!

Picture the scene now, as the Guard Commander, oblivious of the

chaos he has created, marches smartly forward, gives his sword salute and proudly shouts the traditional invitation: '*No 2 Flying Training School Guard of Honour ready for your inspection, Sir!*' The response from AVM Atcherley was a little less conventional, '*When you get that bloody lot sorted out, I'll inspect them!*'

This caused the Flight Lieutenant to 'lose his cool', as, with sword in hand, he looks back over his shoulder and mutters, '*Christ!*'

But he has been told to sort it out, and he returns to face his men. After a pause, during which the contortions on his face revealed the torture in his mind, he issued this unique order: 'When I say *Go*', those at the *Slope* stand fast, those at the *Present* and at the *Order* go to the *Slope*'. '*GO!*'

A rather nervous successor was appointed the next day. And his first duty was . . .

3
The Nineteen Hour Day

I am going to take you on a 'Changi Slip'—and tell some more 'Tales' on the way. But, first, let us understand a component of our journey—the length of our working day—or night—or day and night!

You are flying out of your home base of RAF Lyneham. The aircraft is loaded with its freight, the passengers are assembling—it is three hours to take-off. It might be imagined, by the naive, that the time is 6am, say, for a reasonable start to a long day. But no, it can be any time of day or night! Schedules were devised to allow for factors such as assembly times for passengers and the ideal time for them to arrive at their destination or to ensure an even flow of aircraft along the main route and so on. These factors invariably dictated that departure times were not at a reasonable hour and it was not unusual to start one's day by getting out of bed at say 9pm. It can be imagined the difficulties that this created and I always felt that we were lucky not to have had an accident that could be attributed to crew fatigue. To highlight this comment it should be noted that the 'crew duty day' could, in those days, last for nineteen hours with no compensation for the time of day it started.

Just relate that to a normal working day. The 19 hours were counted from two hours before take-off when the crew would arrive at the airfield to start planning and preparation. So, to ally it to your normal working day, you would arrive at work at 8am, say, be fairly busy for two hours on a variety of tasks, both mental and physical. At 10am would commence a period of fairly intense activity: loading the passengers, start-up and taxy and the take-off and departure. There then follows a period of more relaxed concentration of, say, seven hours of cruising flight. Then comes a build-up in work load with the descent and landing. You have landed at 5.30pm. Working day over? Oh no!

More planning and preparation for an hour and a half and you are concentrating again on the next take-off and departure. You might be lucky—it could be a straightforward departure in good weather. Some hope!

If by now you feel that this has not been your day, there is worse to come. Let's say that, because of bad weather and head winds, this leg takes longer than the first—eight hours. But buck up—it is time for the landing at your final destination—and it is only 3 am!

You're down. Are you tired? Well, just hang on a minute. The Flight Engineer has to brief the ground crew on any snags. The Air Loadmaster has to hand over the load to the Movements Officer. The Navigator has to visit the Meteorological Office and the Captain and Co-pilot visit Operations. The crew that are taking over have to be seen, if possible, for the hand on of any information on the aircraft.

Ready for bed? OK—you are lucky this time, into the bus and it is only half an hour's drive to your accommodation. If all goes well, you could be in bed by 5 am—but you probably won't. By this time you feel like relaxing with a beer or four . . .

Now remember that the day started with a 6.30 am 'get-up', so there was a good chance that you had a reasonable amount of sleep beforehand. Now transfer the situation to a 11 pm departure from base! Anyway you are here now and you can have a rest, in fact there is a regulation to cover the minimum rest that you must have—15 hours! And that is between the time you landed and your next take-off time!

Many saw our lives as glamorous and something of a 'doddle'—but now you know different. But do you? You seem to have fallen asleep in the chair!

4
Aden Bound

Off we go—Eastbound out of Lyneham, our first stop to be El Adem, North Africa. We have a full load—half freight, half passengers. After take-off, for a short while, we have the usual efficient handling by the London air traffic controllers. The international flavour of the flight starts as we cross the Channel and are passed on to the French controllers—they're not on strike this week!

During World War 2 many Polish and Czechoslovakian aircrew escaped from their beleaguered countries and joined the Royal Air Force to contribute considerably towards our victory. Many of them stayed on in the post-war RAF. They were invariably colourful characters. We had a particularly fine gentleman as a Britannia Captain. But he had a habit that distressed us young co-pilots. The international language of the air is English, though this is sometimes difficult to believe! 'Wed' used to enjoy flexing his linguistic muscles on the airways over France and would reply to the controllers in fluent French. Then he would take his turn away from the flight deck. The radio work that immediately followed could be considered an initiative test for the co-pilot who would have to battle with the subsequent rapid transmission from the ground in which the only thing he recognized was the call sign!

There is no doubt that as 'English' as the Poles and Czechs became, they still retained a distinctive radio voice and style. A complete misunder-standing arose one day when one such pilot was testing another pilot's instrument flying standards. This developed into a frustrating business because air traffic control would not allow the aircraft to do what was necessary to complete the test. In desperation, after yet another refusal, the examiner transmits to ATC, ' . . . *Don't you realize I am a Check Pilot.*' Back came the reply, '*I don't care what nationality you are, continue as instructed!*'

Here's a typical Crewroom Tale 'link'. In the fifties a Polish pilot was somewhere in Germany waiting for his aircraft to be refuelled. A courteous young German pilot, by way of conversation, asked him what he had done during the War. '*You see that car park over there,*' mused the Pole, '*I made it!*'

Back to R/T! The pilot's nightmare became a reality for a BOAC Captain in the Persian Gulf when he landed at the wrong airfield! As he turned off the end of the runway he was asked by air traffic, '*What are your intentions?*' Back came the laconic reply, '*Start a chicken farm?*'

A sortie for a large transport aircraft included landing at an airfield close to its home base. At the end of the landing run the aircraft cleared the runway and the co-pilot changed to the ground control frequency and requested taxy instructions. '*What is your position?*', was the reply from ATC. With some disbelief, for they were within clear view of the Tower, the co-pilot explained that they had just cleared the runway. '*Could you be more precise, we do not have you in sight.*' This cannot be true thinks the co-pilot, but patiently embarks on a careful description of the aircraft's location. His voice slows as he realises that he is on the ground frequency for his home base—and because of its close proximity, in spite of the fact the aircraft is on the ground, they can hear him!

To end with radios, we go back to halcyon days—the early route flying years of the Britannia. A Signaller was carried in those days and a lot of the route communications depended on the good old Morse key. A noticeable disadvantage of having a Signaller (there were many compensating advantages—they always were good 'fixers' on the ground) was that the pilots found it difficult to keep in touch with what was going on. The Navigator was working extremely hard, with limited aids, to maintain track. Every half hour he would pass information to the Signaller for transmission, on the position, etc of the aircraft and weather information. They worked very much as a team and the pilots had to 'interfere' if they wanted to stay in the picture.

In conversation before a particular flight, one Signaller confessed, in a discussion on the Morse Code, that for some reason, he found 'sixes' difficult to send; they broke up his smooth flow and rhythm, an essential of good Morse. You learn over the years not to give your compatriots ammunition like that. On the flight the first lot of information that the Navigator passed to the signaller for transmission went something like this:

'Position 05 56N 060 36E at 0430
Flight Level 190
Estimate 03 46N 070 26E at 0530
Endurance 3 hours 36 minutes
Temperature −6
Wind 266 at 36 knots
Cloud 6/8ths at 6000 feet'

Without being irresponsible, the Nav had put a six everywhere he possibly could!

Enough of this digressing—back to the business of eventually getting to Aden.

We cross the South French coast at Nice, then its island-hopping down the west coast of Italy, then the 'toe' at Caraffa. Historical names crop up like Elba, the small rocky island prison for Napoleon. Good transport pilots keep an awareness of their position in relation to suitable airfields for an immediate landing should some drastic emergency occur. A feature of transport flying is that all crew members are periodically examined and categorized; part of that process is the route check where the examiner sits on your shoulder while you do the job. A pilot route checker was so engaged in the area when he decides to test the co-pilots' awareness. *'What's our nearest diversion airfield then Co?'* Pause. *'Um—Elba.' Elba!* ******* *Elba!* ******* *'E Cat!'* They might put radio beacons on small rocky islands but they can't build airfields! The co-pilot had been awarded an instant 'failed' categorization—the dreaded 'E Cat'.

On we go, striking South from Caraffa, across the Mediterranean to the North coast of Africa to the RAF staging post of El Adem, near Tobruk. One could feel sympathy for the people permanently stationed there. It was a sorry place sitting in its dirty desert. The grubbiness reached into every corner—and it was not always hot, or warm even. This seemed to emphasize the awfulness of the place. We are scheduled to be on the ground for 90 minutes to refuel. During that time the pilots and navigator have to complete the part of the planning for the next leg which could not be done before leaving base. That accomplished, there might be time for a quick meal before being on the way again. To achieve this, transport is made available to the crew.

The association of El Adem and crew transport will remind old hands of a story concerning an angry old Captain. It became the habit of some of the servicing crew of El Adem to get on the crew bus outside the dining room and wait until it went out to the aircraft with the aircrew. For some reason it was decided that this practice was to cease. Captain Angry and crew, meal finished, went out to their bus to be taken to the aircraft and there sitting in it was a particularly scruffy airman. Angry blew his top and ordered the airman off. They then waited for the driver ... Yes, they eventually discovered that it was the driver that the Captain had thrown off! A wealth of similar stories surrounded this particular Captain and in later years he denied many, including this one. Had that folk teller been at work again?

Still feeling fresh? Bit tired? Never mind, we're half way through this first day. Off we go to RAF Khormaksar, Aden. It's desert all the way with very few ground aids to navigation so it would seem reasonable to draw a straight line between El Adem and Khormaksar and simply fly along that. But that would take us over Egypt and we are not permitted to overfly that country. Such a ban is a constant factor in transport flying. The routes that can be taken are governed by the state of diplomatic relations. This results in some long standing blocks but can also mean short notice barriers being raised against direct flights. Part of another route to Singapore which was flown later than ours was between Cyprus and the

Persian Gulf. A direct flight necessitated overflying Syria and this was forbidden. The only solution, in order to progress eastwards, was to fly north all the way up to Ankara, east to Tehran then south to the Gulf—three times the distance.

On our flight we have to keep west to fly around the SW corner of the Egyptian boundary—this became known as 'Nasser's Corner'! If it was light as we left the UK it could well by now be starting to get light again! And we land at Khormaksar at 0800 local time.

The heat, even at that time of the morning, is searing. And the cruel sun bounces off the concrete and the sand into our tired red eyes. If you imagine that the deserts of such places are sandy, as in beach, then this is far from the case. In fact it is difficult to distinguish between 'sand', tarmac and concrete. On this inhospitable surface are perched our unimaginative concrete military buildings, seemingly designed with no thought to minimize the harshness of the environment. Although there was the impression that every grain of sand had been compacted, there was still enough at liberty to create, at times, an eye-irritating and obscuring sand storm.

Ignoring the local time, it's the end of a long working day for us, so it's time for a few beers in *Neddy's Bar*. This facility was one of the first recognitions that slip crews required special arrangements if they were to

lead any sort of reasonable way of life. Wing Commander 'Neddy' Pearson, an early OC Flying at Khormaksar decided that there should be a bar facility at the airfield for crews when they landed, no matter what time of the day or night. This watering-hole was affectionately named *Neddy's Bar*, a name that was transferred to similar facilities, elsewhere, in later years.

Perhaps it is appropriate to talk of drink. At the risk of being put in the same bracket as the lady who did 'protest too much', drinking should be seen in its context. Here you had a bunch of blokes separated from their families (for better, for worse), thrown together for a period of time—and I mean together. There were individuals who could survive in their own company—and they are to be admired for it—but the vast majority needed other people, or, as in my case, relished the company of others when we were forced to make the most of what could easily develop into a maudlin situation. As has been said, many saw our lives as glamorous and envied us, but the truth is that much of the time things could be tedious and uncomfortable unless you made the most of it. The ingredients that most aided this process were drink and companionship.

Refreshed at *Neddy's* we move to our accommodation at *Merifield House*, another early effort which acknowledged the difficulties of route flying and fatigue. It was at Khormaksar that the first signs appeared that

special accommodation arrangements were required for slip crews. They could not just be pushed into any old transit block. They needed reasonable comfort in air-conditioned rooms to help alleviate the transition between climes and time zones. They needed the opportunity to eat and rest at all times of the day and night—and they needed the facility to be 'social' at non-standard times. At Khormaksar the special accommodation built was named *Merifield House* after a past Station Commander. I remember well the first enthusiastic Sergeant Steward who ran the place. One of his dreams was to have a grass area between the buildings, not an easy objective in the middle of a desert. His enthusiasm at organising exceeded his horticultural talents for he had, flown out in a Britannia, the only lawn mower in Aden before a blade of grass had grown there.

I will now let you rest at 'salubrious' RAF Khormaksar and we will continue our journey later.

5
Next Stop Gan, Then Singapore!

We have had a couple of days off at RAF Khormaksar and are scheduled to take on the next aircraft which is due in at I am local time. We had better get to bed at around 5 pm or so, in order to get our sleep. We are on our way—we have enjoyed, as best we can, our few days in Khormaksar. We went to the beach one day. It seems strange to talk of beach on the edge of a desert, but it was there. The most important facility that it possessed was the reed covered structures which provided shade. It was so hot in Aden that it was quite positively injurious to walk barefoot on the sand. Therefore you had to make special footwear arrangements to go for a swim in the luke-warm sea. The hazards also included sharks and a net had been installed to prevent 'mixed bathing'!

Back to the bed you were in, attempting to sleep, more than likely unsuccessfully. The time approaches for your call, part of the route system. It was always assumed, along with all sorts of other shortcomings, that Transport crews were incapable of one, if not both, of the following:

1. Being able to afford or willing to purchase an alarm clock.
2. Being able to set it to the time at which it was necessary to wake.

Because of this extraordinary lack, a most elaborate system had become established whereby a form had to be completed detailing the times and rooms to be called. Part of the task of the eternal 24 hour staff was to ensure that those so listed were called. But there was a bonus to this lumbering system from which you are about benefit. If you were using an alarm clock it would sound off completely oblivious of outside events. However, your manual call system, controlled by the Duty Receptionist, an RAF Sergeant or Corporal with his local minions, is in touch with the

airfield operations room. The message from them is that the aircraft is delayed—do not call the crew! You will no doubt appreciate, from the previous outline of the crew duty day, how important it was to keep them from starting their 'day'. So the picture now is that you went to bed at 5 pm—the time is now past midnight and you have been lucky; you've slept and you are ready to go. In fact you have slept so well that you have woken of your own accord, switched on the light and there, slipped under your door, is a piece of paper with a message—'Aircraft delayed 24 hours'. What do you do now? You are wide awake, ready to go—and it's half past midnight—and with a 24 hour delay there is every prospect of repeating the performance next day!

It is easy for us on these pages to just leap forward 24 hours and get airborne out of Khormaksar before heading across the Indian Ocean to the island staging post of RAF Gan. It is dark—as dark as the proverbial black hole. There are limited aids to navigation. The navigator will be working hard, relying on his Doppler equipment, monitored by astro-shots. Every half-hour he will have to do quite an elaborate calculation with figures obtained from the 'Air Almanac'. Then he'll be up at the sextant looking for the stars on which he has based his computation. Concentration is high as he presses his eye to the rubber shrouded eye piece. With so much to think about he will not be aware that a wit has put

some sort of blacking on the rubber so by the end of his session with the sextant we have a navigator with a black eye! The games aircrew play! It's all done in the best of fun and does help to lift spirits. Prime jokers are usually the Air Quartermasters. Up they will come on to the flight deck with the crew drinks in paper cups on a tray. Just inside the door on the left sits the signaller—and the 'Q' performs an elaborate trip over some imaginary obstacle as he enters. With a cascade of paper cups heading his way, the signaller moves as much as he can, which is not far. He is covered—in the torn up bits of paper that were in the cups! But beware Quartermaster—the next joke is likely to be on you!

On this Indian Ocean route, communications used to be very poor. The Signaller would spend hours trying to pass messages either by voice or Morse to ground control. At the risk of seeming racist, Karachi always presented great problems, as did Colombo. On this particular

frustrating night the Signaller had been calling and calling 'Karachi, Karachi, Karachi, this is Rafair 6210, do you read, over.' To vent some of his frustration he transmitted 'Come on you stupid brown bastard, answer me'. Back came an immediate reply from a very offended Asian.

We are heading towards Gan, the southern-most of the Maldivian chain of islands, the original purpose-built staging post. It was small: the runway occupied the whole length and much of the rest was occupied by the necessary buildings. To indicate size, it was possible, though something of an endurance test in the heat, to walk around the island in an hour. It was a coral atoll with a lagoon. To build the airfield it was necessary to destroy almost every form of tree and plant. But as a result of prodigious growth rate and a deliberate restoration policy, it was not long before the trees and greenery regrew to create a contradictory environment—a 100 per cent military establishment in a tropical paradise. Firstly little need be said about the tropical paradise. The sun shone, the temperatures soared but there was always a sea breeze; the palm trees swayed, the sands glistened white and the sea was an unbelievable blue. But into this setting you had, as if dropped by some supernatural parachute, an RAF station with its runway, dispersal area, control tower, engineering and administrative buildings and accommodation. But this would not have felt so uncanny in such an idyllic setting had it not been for one thing —no women! Only men were posted to Gan and the married ones had to leave their families in the UK. This was the scene of the ultimate in 'unaccompanied tours', which were for one year. A jealously guarded acquisition of these deprived men was the Gan tie which said it all:

To say there were no women is an injustice to the two 'welfare' ladies on the island. In this male fortress they ran clubs, libraries and the like on behalf of the Malcolm Clubs organization and the Women's Royal Voluntary Service. There were also in transit, like all aircrew, the female Air Quartermasters—but more of them later.

Operating into such a location did present its problems. It was incredibly small and difficult to find, albeit that it did have a powerful radio beacon to home on to in the latter stages of the flight. But this facility was in the category of a reassurance. One must admire the skill of the navigators of that time who took great pride in maintaining a precise track despite the sparse wind information and the complete lack of other navigational aids. It never ceased to impress me that as you proceeded across the Indian Ocean some 1800 miles or more that, having made radio contact with a Britannia on the reverse route, you invariably were able to see that aircraft bound in the opposite direction. That's precise navigation! Having painted a holiday brochure picture of the island's weather it was necessary not to mention the tropical thunderstorms. These could be horrendous, but it was proved, statistically, that their duration was such that aircraft could hold off for sufficient time for the storms to clear. Nevertheless accidents did occur. A civil Britannia undershot the runway, a Victor departed from the runway as did an RAF Britannia. The latter incident did not involve a standard squadron pilot but one a little higher in the promotion ladder who retired as an Air Chief Marshal! We all learnt about aqua-planing from that event but little about getting promoted! He said in later years, how many hairy old Flight Lieutenants subsequently said to him how they had had a close shave in the ice rink situation created by a very wet runway and the high speed tyre of a landing aircraft. But with a wipe of the brow, they had forgotten about it. Potential Air Chief Marshals do not let such things pass and the hazard was fully investigated and techniques evolved to overcome it.

In an environment like Gan, legends flourished. It was said that there was a once domesticated monkey running wild on the island. It had been teased a lot and was out to seek revenge. So beware if you were sitting on the loo, trousers around ankles, and a hairy arm came under the door—it was only after one thing! The monkey was all in the mind but fruit bats were not. They hung in the trees most of the time but at dusk they took to the air—pedestrians beware. They did have dirty habits. While we are in this lavatorial mood, let me mention the crabs. It was alleged, over the years at different locations, that a crab had settled in the sewers where it had flourished and grown to an enormous size. It was very agile and roamed from loo to loo—the mind boggles!

There was a tremendous camaraderie on Gan. The permanent staff seemed to resign themselves to being away from their loved ones and decided to make the most of it. There were constant touches of humour. An ATC controller would pass an incredibly complex departure instruction to an aircraft entitled the 'Hittadu Two Departure' or something similar—this in a flying environment with no restrictions whatever. There was leg-pulling humour for visiting crews—there is many the newcomer, looking for the nightlife, who has been sent off in search of 'The Golden Flip-Flop'! On the reception desk of the Transit Hotel, there was an electric bell-push marked 'Please ring for attention'—but if you lifted it and investigated, it wasn't connected to anything at all!

Gan was, within the constraints of the all-male situation, a very social place and we crews passing through played our part. I remember a period when I decided that a good route flying pastime would be to learn to play

the guitar. My idea was to practise in the privacy of my room—but come late at night I would be persuaded to bring out the guitar and give it a strum—I never did get past the strumming stage. On hearing the first chord, voices would be raised in song. I was supposed to be playing an accompaniment—very flattering but I could have been playing anything, as the singers were well away. After one such evening I was wending my way to bed—with a bicycle. Bikes were provided for crew use; a ride around the island was a favourite pastime. That is what I intended doing the next day and I was being devious by taking a bike to my room to ensure availability in the morning. As I rode along in the dark, guitar under arm, I could hear music coming through the tropical night. Even though it was very late I was drawn as the moth to the flame! Homing in on the sound I came upon the Sergeants' Mess. My normal good judgement and decorum must have been somewhat impaired for I rode into the main entrance, along the verandah and into the bar. A cheer went up as I parked my bike. I was obviously a happy addition to the musical evening. I stopped my hosts mid-welcome and said that they might be pleased to see me but I really shouldn't be in the Sergeants' Mess and perhaps I should put things straight with the obviously senior members at the bar. At this point the assembled throng, to a man, suggested that I put it right with this gentleman first, pointing to the Station Commander!

An incredible phenomena at Gan was the local labour force. None of them were permitted to live on the island. It was part of their terms of service that they left for their home island each evening and returned the following morning. This produced the most incredible sight at sunset as a flotilla of dhows, each containing between 20 and 30 men, were rowed away from the beach. On a bad day some of them could be rowing for a couple of hours only to do the return journey a few hours later. They were a cheerful people—but we contaminated a lot of their naturalness. We gave them a taste for Western goods. They even bought motorbikes when there were only the shortest of tracks on each island. But we did improve their standard of living and health, so much so that the women started bearing larger children which provided difficulties at birth. This was one of the reasons why the two resident RAF doctors had to be a surgeon and an anaesthetist.

The Maldivian lads acquired a lot of our sayings and some of our sense of humour. In the dining room one day one of the waiters came to the table obviously having had an accident with a bowl of soup, which he had spilt down his white jacket. One of the diners remarked to him that he was obviously not Number One (the Far East term for the head waiter). 'No sir, me number 49!' It should be a cause for concern as to what happened to all those people, with their changed standards and dependence on Britain, when the RAF vacated the island.

Time to move on to Singapore—more precisely RAF Changi. Again, more than likely a night flight; in fact as I remember it, we always seemed to be flying over Sumatra and down the Straights to Singapore Island just as the sun was rising—straight into our tired eyes. Accompanying this was the change to Singapore air traffic controllers who were incredibly efficient but spoke so fast. To heighten your awareness of tiredness there was a fairly precise descent route that had to be flown to bring you out, lined up with the runway at Changi. In fact there was need for caution

here because as you came around the last beacon and looked up there were two runways ahead—Changi's and the one at Paya Lebar, Singapore's international airport. A tired crew once took the wrong one and it was not until they had touched down that they were aware of their error. But a more disastrous mistake could have followed when the Captain started applying power to take-off again. He was restrained by the Engineer who realised that, at the prevailing weight and temperature, insufficient runway remained.

You have reached your resting place for this chapter—the Transit Hotel, Royal Air Force Changi. So enjoy the sun, though you will find it a bit sticky. And don't spend too much money on 'bargains' in Changi Village. Eat 'Chinese' when you can, but don't drink too much *Tiger Beer*. I'll start taking you home in the next chapter.

6
Half way—and Time for a Rest and Some 'Tales'

In a successful crew one of most important ingredients, on what was technically a complex aircraft, was the bond between Captain and Engineer. In the early days of the Britannia a fixed crew system, inherited from the Hastings fleet, was operated. When this was abolished, to give greater flexibility, it was still considered important that the Captain and Engineer should still be paired. After a while of operating the random crew system, as often happens in these matters, a new Squadron CO decided to revert to the constituted crew scheme. It was seen that the fairest way of doing this was to place a list of the Captains' names on a board and ask individuals to nominate with whom they would like to fly. The list had to be taken down when it became evident that Captains F, J, M and Z were not going to have any volunteers. It should have been a salutary lesson for them. This reflected a situation with the constituted crew system where there was always, at the bottom of the league, about four crews in a constant state of flux. These were manned by those people who would come back from a particular trip saying they would never fly with Captain Bloggs again—so they were swapped with another crew member who complained about Captain Prune! I was lucky in my early co-pilot days for I was with a good bunch, my ex-Royal New Zealand Air Force Captain shielded me from the cruel world whilst I got the hang of flying, what seemed to be then, this giant aircraft.

Engineer types ranged from the practical sort, who would be oil up to the ears and carrying every tool and odd spare part, to the theoretical, clerical type who would work in white gloves and leave all the dirty stuff to the appropriate people. There was a particular 'oily' engineer who was also clumsy. One day he settled into his hotel room and decided to have a shower. All was set, temperature adjusted and he steps into the bath—

and slips. He grabs the shower curtain to save himself—and pulls it off the wall. The curtain rail falls on the wash-basin and cracks off an enormous piece of porcelain. This falls on the toilet and breaks it from top to bottom! In seconds the bathroom has been vandalized. Our rather large, but sheepish, gentle Engineer gets dressed and seeks out the Hotel Manager. This takes a while, which gives him time to think. By the time the Manager appears, aggression has been gathered and sheepish, gentle Engineer goes into the attack and complains about slippery bath bottoms and the near fatal accident he has just had. But can you imagine the scene as the Manager surveys the bathroom?

A word about another crew member of those days. The engineers were a particularly well established bunch, both as an aircrew category and, in the case of the Britannia, their individual experience. The aircraft was particularly demanding on the engineer's technical ability and only the best and more experienced were chosen. Without being unkind the same could not be said of the Air Quartermasters—this I hasten to add—

through no fault of their own. Their aircrew category was not long established (in fact when the Britannia first came into service, the trade did not exist). Men from ground trades, principally suppliers, were seconded to flying duties for a period. They did well and established the need for a professional band with their expertise lying in loading and trimming the aircraft and caring for the passengers and crew.

It did mean that when the AQM brevet was instigated there were many anomalies at the start. Those seconded at the time found themselves several ranks higher as the rules for aircrew promotion were applied. The new recruits, who started as Sergeants, seemed very fresh-faced. This caused a much wartime bemedalled Canadian Customs Officer to remark to one young man, 'You're a Sergeant? Christ! You must have been born a Corporal!'

And then came the ladies—the first females to wear a Royal Air Force flying brevet. That must have rustled a few feathers in the Air Ministry. But they were a great success. To begin with it was considered that they had been essentially recruited to cover the families' air trooping aspect of our work, but we rapidly found out that they were not prepared to be confined in this way. The 'Air Quartermistresses', as they hated being called, wanted to, and did, play an equal role. But they were different (!) and it was most noticeable how they raised the tone of the crew with whom they were flying. Naturally there were 'liaisons'—many happy, some sad.

Stays at Changi were always pleasant. We again had our dedicated accommodation—the Changi Creek Hotel. This was a sprawl of buildings set by the inlet to the shopping area, Changi Village. To and fro each day would chug boats carrying merchandise and shoppers from outlying islands. Smaller craft were rowed in that strange standing-up, looking forward stance. Fishermen patrolled the shore with their rolled up nets which they cast out on the surface of the water with a flick of the wrist and with sufficient speed to trap the fish beneath.

The hub of the accommodation was a traditional Far Eastern building which was originally the Japanese Officers' Mess during the occupation. In the main public room was a large fish tank. For a while it bore a notice, 'The Anemone Fish in this tank were given by members of 216 Squadron'. A continual rivalry existed between us and the Comet crews of 216 Squadron with whom we shared the Singapore route. It was thus that, after a while, a second note appeared on the tank, 'The Achilles Angelfish, which ate the Anemone Fish presented by 216 Squadron, were presented by 511 Squadron.' So one of the Britannia Squadrons had struck. The rivalry between the Comets and Britannias was exceeded by that between the two Britannia Squadrons—'*The Long Hogbacked Goatfish, which ate the Achilles Angelfish ... 511 Squadron ... which ate ... Anemone Fish ... 216 Squadron was presented by 99 Squadron.*' The management called a halt when there were a considerable number of cards on the side of the tank and all it contained, in the murky water, was the gift of the last donor—a huge skulking catfish caught in the Creek outside!

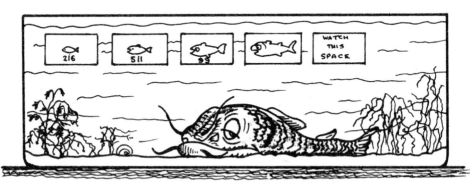

Singapore is a sticky place. The sun beats down—and does it rain—so the humidity is always quite high. The sun was a particular hazard to some aircrew of those early days. Ideas on pilot fitness have changed over the years. When I first joined the Royal Air Force it seemed that the feeling was that you would drop dead if you flew over the age of forty! There were also strict rules about eyesight. It was virtually unheard of for a pilot to fly with spectacles. Consequently, those of advancing years whose eyesight was on the decline were reluctant to declare their disability. To overcome this some pilots used a magnifying glass! But this had to be utilized with care in Changi for if used for too long to study some document or other in the sun, ignition could occur!

Alongside us 'big boys' on the dispersals of these staging posts would be the local short range transport aircraft. At Changi these were the Argosys of which many an unkind remark was made of its performance. '*It's payload is the cargo floor!*' '*It CAN carry something—a verbal message?*'.

Fast-forward in time for a small Argosy digression—to my time at Boscombe Down, where it was the habit for we staff pilots to be used as co-pilots in aircraft with which we were not at all familiar. 'Sandbags' we were called, which clearly indicated our dormant role. Dave X was despatched to the Argosy outside to settle himself in the right hand seat before the arrival of the rest of the crew. His first difficulty was finding the

way in. The aircraft was obviously ready for flight but all the doors were firmly shut. Then he discovers the small hatch that looked like part of the nose wheel assembly! So he is in—but then there is another difficulty—no flight deck! But then he finds the ladder!

As we are resting, 'Tales' are bound to told. These stories do switch back and forth in time—but that is a feature of Tales from the Crewroom! I can take you back into the depths of time—when I had completed my pilot training. We really thought we were something then—we had escaped from Flying Training Command and were now in FIGHTER COMMAND, about to start our Day Fighter OCU course on Meteors! Phew!

On Day One we were soon put in our place. The Wing Commander Flying ruled by tyranny; nobody seems to do that any more as they have more subtle methods. He had the misfortune to have a stutter, but this did not prevent him from delivering a torrent of threats and abuse—it just took him longer. He had pet hates. Heaven help the Pilot Officer who fell asleep in the Mess Ante-Room after lunch. Also we were not allowed to sit in comfort in the Crewroom. We were hauled outside to '*Watch the aircraft, you might learn something.*' The first trip we did was a Sector Recce, where we found our way around unfamiliar East Anglia. I was foolish enough, for reassurance, to call Air Traffic Control for a 'True Bearing'. There was obviously a 'spy' in the tower for I was hauled before the Wing Commander and told at some length that 'big boys' did not do such things on a Sector Recce in Fighter Command!

Oddly, he did not always stutter on the R/T. We assumed that, by careful timing, he used up his opening burst of vocal disability before pressing the TRANSMIT button and so passed his message clearly. However, as his rate of stutter increased in direct proportion to his loss of temper, there were occasions when this technique did not work. One day he broke into Stradishall circuit, fuming and spluttering about something or other—and suffered a total runaway stutter. Meteors fell helplessly about the skies, as they listened to Mac's attempts at R/T in the circuit. His message came over as, *'SSSSS .. SStradusga ga ga gakk .. BBBBBlack One .. DDDown ... dddown ... downwi ... we .. w ... FF FFFine ... FFine ... FFinal ... FF ... Oh! *** it! Round again!'*

A contemporary of mine recalled the end of his course there.

'For my last flight, on the OCU course, I was honoured to fly as Mac's No 2 on a day when it was snowing like the clappers. He didn't believe in all this bloody R/T chat and hadn't said a word to me throughout the sortie. I stuck to him like the proverbial to a blanket, knowing that to get lost and call for a steer meant an automatic weekend as Orderly Officer. We ended up doing a pairs landing on a very slippery runway. My Meteor thumped in, fully stalled, on the lip of the runway, so I had no problem about stopping. But Mac didn't quite negotiate the turn-off at the end and skidded sideways into the outfield in a flurry of snow. Air Traffic held their breath and not a word was said. As I taxied gingerly past the purple-faced OC Flying, I politely enquired on the R/T if he needed assistance. I cringed back to dispersal under his instructions to, *"PPPP*** off, SSSmSSmSmart Arse!"* Next day, I went to his office—Best Blue and Bates Hat job—to collect my log book, wherein he had written his comments on my abilities as a Meteor day-fighter pilot before my posting to Tangmere. I was distressed to read his assessment of "Overconfident" recorded on the F414A. I plucked up courage to ask him politely if he would elaborate on this rather cutting and potentially damaging assessment. Flying Wing Adj almost fainted. The Wing Commader glared at me, grabbed my log-book, wrote something in it, slammed it shut and thrust it back into my trembling hands. I'm willing to bet that I'm one of the few pilots to have an OCU assessment of *"Overconfident GIT."*'

We shared RAF Stradishall with another unit that had some really old people in it. Well, they seemed old then—but on reflection they were probably 20 years younger than I am now. To us youngsters, anyone more than 30 was definitely over the hill. Amongst these ancients was a short fat Flight Lieutenant who was notorious for two things—the amount of beer he consumed and eggs. Yes, eggs. He lived in the Mess during the week, but at weekends he went somewhere where there was this stock of eggs, which were worth his while bringing back to Stradishall to sell. So, on Monday his room resembled more an Egg Market than a place to sleep.

This particular Monday evening Short Fat Flight Lieutenant (SFFL) is in his customary corner of the Bar at his customary time—early. We young blades, with our matching appetites, had our Dinner first and by the time we went for a drink, SFFL was well away. He did not last long—possibly still tired from all that weekend egg gathering—and off he staggered to bed. We should not have scoffed at his condition for we were doing our best to emulate it—and then it became 'playing silly tricks' time.

The potential of a very soundly asleep SFFL in a room full of eggs occurred to someone . . .

It is amazing how quiet a rowdy bunch can become when up to no good—we decided to stealthily enter SFFL's room and carefully spread the eggs all over his floor. This was duly done. The master touch was to remove the bulb from his bedside lamp as we crept out—filling the path with more eggs as we went.

All is set, no corridor lights—it is pitch black. Gentle 'Knock, knock'—all very subtle, but very persistent—until SFFL is roused.

Still 'Knock, knock', but now with a garbled message. There is a fumbling for the ineffective bedside light switch. Eventually he is persuaded to come to his door. Bare feet—eggs—squelch, squelch!! You, knowing the situation, would cut your losses and either make a straight line for the door or turn around and go back to bed! SFFL is not possessed with your good sense or detachment and dodges about all over the room trying to escape from the squelch, squelch!

Once started these 'Tales' cannot stop—and that's how it used to be as we whiled away our days at Changi. Mention has been made of pilot assessment entries in log books—which reminds me! More will be told later of the considerable amount of time and effort expended by the Britannia fleet following Rhodesia's Unilateral Declaration of Independence (UDI), flying oil from East Africa into a marooned Zambia. During this period it became time for we pilots to submit our log books to our CO for his annual assessment of our ability to be entered therein. This is a yearly routine for all RAF pilots but in our case was something of a formality as the appraisal given would relate to the 'category' that we held from our various flying tests: 'C', average—'B', above average and so on. One of my compatriots was somewhat taken aback, as the holder of a 'B' category, to find that his entry read 'average' and passed his log book back to the Squadron Adjutant for the error to be corrected. My fellow

Captain quickly found out that the mistake was his! The Boss's summons was immediate—the entry was not a mistake. It related to the fact that Dave had been driving around for the past months with a 'Support Rhodesia' sticker in the back window of his car!

This particular guy did have an inclination to upset CO's. On another occasion he was co-pilot to his CO Captain and they were at Gander, Newfoundland in its large 'white elephant' air terminal. The Wing Commander was looking his dignified best as there was a VIP due through at the same time and he knew him from the past. But his flight planning activities had to proceed and it came time to visit the Met Office upstairs. The co-pilot led the way up a stationary escalator—he pulled ahead, his CO being only half-way up when Dave reaches the top—where, for some inexplicable reason (at least it was subsequently) he pressed the escalator 'go down' button. His leader had a great deal of difficulty maintaining his dignified appearance whilst continuing to try to make his way upwards!

Let us make one more trip down a story lane by considering the topic of 'forbidden words'.

Well after my RAF Britannia days, I was posted to the Aeroplane and Armament Experimental Establishment, Boscombe Down to fly their Britannia, a 300 series. This led to flying other types there. One day, whilst in the Comet, we were talking to the aircraft for which we were acting as target and to the ground radar station. In this situation it might be necessary to speak to each of the other 'stations' in turn and the convention is to define who you are talking to by using the word 'Break', at the appropriate point in the message, when you switch from one station to the other.

'Echo 2 from Evergreen XX, estimating on task at 1151, BREAK, Eastmer Radar, Evergreen XX maintaining Flight Level 190.'
'Evergreen XX this is Eastmer Radar, Roger. Do not use the word BREAK on air-to-air refuelling frequencies.'

What we innocents had done in this unfamiliar world, in which air-to-air refuelling sorties took place, was use a 'FORBIDDEN WORD'! Forbidden words largely arise out of myth and legend. In this case it would be alleged that, once upon a time, a receiver aircraft, taking fuel from a tanker, had heard the word 'Break' used in the context above and thought it was an order for him to break contact with the refuelling hose! The admonishing controller above, in his eagerness to display his superiority had, of course, compounded our offence by using the word himself! But more on this theme later.

The 'forbidden word'—and how obtuse its associated reasoning can be—is probably best illustrated with the prohibited use of 'colour' words when on parachuting sorties. You may well be aware that a red light means 'get ready' and a green, 'jump'. It is alleged that, one day, on such a flight, one of the flight deck crew said, in one of those casual conversations that do take place, '*Look at that red house down there with the green roof*'— and all the paratroopers jumped out of the aircraft! So it continues to this day—woe betide the co-pilot—and it usually is the co-pilot—who, on a parachuting sortie, mentions a colour over the intercomm!

Another area of 'words' is the abandoned take-off by large aircraft, where a decision is made before a calculated speed, whether or not to continue the take-off. Crew members 'suggest' to the Captain that the take-off should be abandoned, because of some fault they have noticed, by the use of a chosen 'word'. This word has varied over the years. To begin with it was 'Reject', but myth and legend struck and the story is told that 'reject' came to be transmitted over the air and an overflying fighter pilot, thinking he had heard the word 'Eject', fired himself out of the aircraft on his ejector seat!

So the word became 'forbidden' and was substituted by 'Stop'. This did not last long, for some reason, and was replaced by—wait for it ladies— 'ABORT'! This unfortunate word has stood the test of time.

Years ago, around the time of these changes, there was, on 99 Squadron, a rather strange Air Engineer—not worthy of comment, I hear you say. But this chap had an unfortunate affliction. In spite of being quite clever and completely competent at his job, he did give the impression, due to some medical condition, that he was permanently drunk! In fact he used to carry a card, signed by the Medical Officer, to certify that he was not inebriated!

On this particular day, Captain Cool was starting his take-off run at Nairobi, notorious—because of its high altitude—for a very slow acceleration during take-off. This had just commenced and the aircraft was barely moving when the Engineer of wild-eyed appearance, lacking in limb coordination and with slurred speech, noticed something amiss. His hands were waving, his lips were moving, but nothing was coming forth! The Captain—Cool by name and cool by nature—turned to the Engineer, '*The word you are looking for, Eng, is ABORT!*' '*That's the ******* word!*', he cries, with which the throttles were closed and he goes into his full 'abort' drill, which includes selecting full reverse on the engines. But, in spite of the lapse of time for all the foregoing to have taken place, the aircraft is still only going fairly slowly. But the Engineer, overcome by the recent events, relaxes and before long, with the deliberate inattention of the Captain, the aircraft is trundling backwards! The Engineer leaps back into life and cancels reverse!

Let us consider a final word—MARK!—familiar to maritime crews, and a 'forbidden word', for, on this call, whilst on patrol, a smoke float is released to mark a point for later reference. Captain Obnoxious was in charge on this day—and he had lived up to his name so far—and the aircraft had only just reached its patrol area over the sea. Something was spotted by the Captain and he rattled out the standard cry, '*MARK, MARK, contact 10 o'clock*'—an indication to the rather ancient crew member manning the look out position on the Port side of the aircraft that he should drop a smoke float. Port Beam had had enough—he had been a particular target for Captain Obnoxious' attention and he did not want to play any more.

Obnoxious is fuming, '*Port Beam, why didn't you drop a float when I called MARK?*' '*Float gone, Port beam*', comes the laconic response. '*Negative, Port Beam. I was only talking about MARK ...*' '*Float gone, Port Beam.*'

Captain Obnoxious is losing control—'*Port Beam, do not launch any more floats when I am only speaking about MARK ...*' Master AEOp Obtuse drones, '*Float gone, Port Beam.*'

Final Score: Captain Obnoxious Nil, MAEOp Obtuse 8. They couldn't play any more as the floats had all been expended!

Before all this tale telling, you may recall that we were 'resting' at RAF Changi, on Singapore Island. We were not generally very adventurous sightseers. Very quickly after starting route flying, seeing new places became quite commonplace. Excuses could be made that our rest time was important and we should not spend the time galloping around seeing the sights. There was the climate—and finance came into it, too. But it was mostly sheer laziness, as our needs were satisfied on our doorstep.

One trip out though, in Singapore, was to eat 'Chinese'. In the sixties this involved a foray to Bedok Corner. Here the stalls were set out with the squid, octopus and less indentifiable objects hanging up in the light of strong paraffin lamps. There was one stall holder who captured nearly all the 'slip crew' market, Mr Lim. He was always so pleased to see you, so enthusiastic and hard working. I can picture him now taking the order, sending a small boy off for the cold beers, then crouching on the ground with a simple flame under his trusty wok, rapidly preparing all manner of dishes.

His washing-up method was intriguing; it consisted of seven buckets of water. The dishes were dipped in each one in turn, always in the same order, the theory being that the water and the dish gradually became cleaner. I reckoned that the first bucket in the sequence became the 'Soup of the Day' the next evening.

Bedok Corner, in true Singapore land reclamation style, disappeared in time and Mr Lim moved up to Changi Village. So for many the one and only reason for going into the City was removed.

That's it—full of *Tiger Beer*—sweet and sour pork hopefully staying down—time to return to Changi Creek Hotel and bed. We're homeward bound in the morning.

7
Farewell Singapore

Our aircraft is serviceable and we are up early on to the ubiquitous white aircrew coach—they seem to wait for us around the world. Now will be revealed the purchases made during our stay in 'shopping bargains' country by our compatriots—the good sense of their buys inflated now by a deflation in their minds of the purchase price. First we go to the aircraft to load our kit and all these goods and then there is a split: the Engineer and Air Quartermaster (or should I now say Air Loadmaster as we have now moved forward a few years) remain at, or in the vicinity of, the aircraft and the Captain, Co-pilot and Navigator go to Operations, the Meteorological Office and Flight Planning.

The weather in this region is of great significance. Crossings of the Indian Ocean can range from the innocuous to the mortifying. The Met man had little information to go on. One of his major sources, of course, was inbound crews. An important factor for Britannia crews was the forecast air temperatures at the cruising heights. The Britannia suffered, during its early days, a tremendous engine icing problem. It was quite an unknown factor and delayed the aircraft's entry into commercial airline service until a protective system was devised. In fact two systems were developed, one used mainly by the RAF called 'cowl heat' and the civil version known by the quaint title 'B Skin Jets'. Strangely we in the Royal Air Force were convinced that we had the cheap-skate version. In later years I learnt this was not so. When I ended my Britannia days flying the Boscombe Down aircraft, a 300 series civil version, I learnt that its engine icing performance was much worse than that of the RAF fleet.

What we were stuck with was some sort of atmospheric juggling act. We could not, if we were to operate safely within our fuel margins, fly at a height that gave us an air temperature of between $+2°C$ and $+12°C$, as registered on a gauge that read the temperature outside the aircraft. In that range in cloud, we had to switch on the cowl heat to prevent the engines accumulating ice in their air intakes. Because of the power absorbed by the system this equated to the loss of one engine. Furthermore, if we were in the temperature range of $+2°C$ to $+6°C$ we had to reduce speed to 200 knots.

All this led to a lot of concentration when flight planning in the tropics. Incidentally, just to complete this engine icing saga, if the above limitations were ignored or indeed observed, but in conditions so critical that the cowl heat could not cope, then the first indication would be engine 'bumping'. This alarming phenomenon was caused by lumps of ice forming in the intake, then becoming detached and going through the engine! The next stage, if one was foolhardy enough—or forced—to remain in those conditions, was the 'auto-relight'. This was the long-stop that the engine manufacturers had provided. If so much ice went through the engine that the flame was extinguished altogether there was a plug glowing red hot to re-ignite the fuel and get the engine restarted. Imagine yourself as a passenger. It is dark, you are in cloud, the engines have been making some strange noises. Suddenly there is a definite lurch as one of the engines suddenly loses all power. Then the night sky is illuminated by a 30 foot long flame from the back of the engine—an auto-relight!

Now summon up some more courage because there is another stage beyond auto-relight if the glow plug has failed to relight the engine. As the engine rpm dies away one of the crew has to carry out a manual engine restart known as the 'rapid relight' drill! Knowing these things helps concentrate the mind on deciding what height and which route to fly. Our other torment was cumulo-nimbus clouds, worldwide always a nasty, with the capability in the extreme of aircraft break-up, but particularly in this part of the world where they realise their maximum potential in terms of turbulence, lightning and icing.

You'll enjoy it when we get to Gan—that is if the one in ten chance of a thunderstorm overhead at our landing time does not occur . . .

Off we go on a deliberately scheduled night departure as the temperature would be too high during the day for us to take-off safely at our weight on the length of runway available at Changi. Having considered all the awful things that could happen let's make it an anti-climax. It is a lovely night and the weather is clear all the way back to Gan. We are only going to refuel there this time, so after just 90 minutes on the ground we are off again to Bahrein. The airfield there is a joint military and civil facility and the RAF element is called Muharraq.

Bahrein is one of those typical Middle Eastern states where poverty, dirt and decrepitude rub shoulders with wealth, modernity and extravagance. In summer the heat borders on the unbearable. As a result of all this very few crew members venture outside our dedicated air conditioned accommodation, appropriately named *Britannia House*. To match our needs it is a 24 hour a day operation. The instant aircrew liquid refreshment facility, in acknowledgement of the founding Catering Officer, Flight Lieutenant Cass, goes by the name of *The Cass Bar*. Geddit?

We were not always so lucky. In the early days we were inadequately accommodated in huts behind the Officers' Mess at RAF Muharraq itself. I remember this being the scene of a startling and unusual experience. Over the subsequent years I was able to make capital out of this by pointing out to successive crew mates, as we drove past the Guardroom, that I had spent a night in the cells there!

It came about through that devil, drink, and its adverse effect on one of my compatriots. It is strange the range of behaviour that one can meet as certain nights wear on. At one end of the scale is the chap who just mellows and mellows—at the other end is the violent fighter. On this night there was some excuse as we had endured a long and tiring 24 hours being flown out to Bahrein as passengers to operate an aircraft at a later date. Unfortunately we arrived just at evening bar opening time. Unbeknown to my fellow crew member, in this duty-free environment, doubles were the standard measure. I wandered off to bed early and slept well until I was woken by my Captain who told me that Flying Officer X had gone berserk and finally had to be restrained by the RAF Police who had no choice but to lock him in a cell.

The delicacy of Royal Air Force Law dictates that, in such circumstances, an officer should be present to 'guard' the prisoner. As the humble co-pilot, I had won the major prize!

Down at the Guardroom I was shown my, by now, sleeping responsibility and my bed for the night—a mattress beside him on the cell floor. With that it was the traditional '*Mind your fingers—Clang!*'. But I was so tired, I was soon asleep.

Can you imagine those first few waking moments with the sun blazing through the cell window? Having gathered my thoughts, the next realization was that I desperately needed to go to the lavatory. 'Ring bell for attention'. Keys rattled, the door was opened slightly and a concerned looking Corporal peeped in. '*I need to go to the loo*', said I. Now I know that I too had had a bad night, but not bad enough surely to prompt his reply. '*Are you the prisoner or the escort, Sir?*'

This took place in my eager co-pilot days. The system was that, with few exceptions, pilots, when they joined the Britannia fleet, started as co-pilots. This was an excellent idea and proved to be the only sensible way to introduce someone to the complexities of operating this sophisticated aircraft. They served in this role for two to three years when, providing that they had sufficiently impressed, they did a short conversion course to CAPTAIN! It is a strange fact of the aircrew world that these two roles— Captain, Co-pilot—are at opposite ends of the status spectrum. A co-pilot is considered to be unaware, ill-informed, and incompetent—the butt of jokes— a situation aggravated by his earnestness. It goes without saying that a Captain is at the opposite end of the scale in a prestigious position. He is respected, for a crew with no outward respect for its Captain has no self respect. It is also a matter of self-preservation to support him, keep him well informed and help him as much as possible! Some blossomed in this situation. Others, perhaps with some personality defect, allowed it to cloud their judgement of self. Whatever type you were flying with, this situation had to be endured. After all it was not going to last forever—it could just seem like it.

Perhaps the situation is best illustrated with a little sub-tale! The location is a huntin', shootin', fishin' area of Canada. An annual visitor there hired everything he needed on the spot—guns, rods, nets—all the accoutrements for the outdoor life. The array would be completed with a dog. He had a regular favourite. It was obedient, worked hard and always willing. This particular year, it is holiday time and our man is hiring his equipment again. All is set and is to be rounded off with the dog. *'I'll have the one I've had these past years.'* The proprietor sighs, *'Well I wouldn't advise that, Sir, you see—that eager willing dog you had, called 'Co-pilot'— since you were last here someone renamed him 'Captain' and now he just sits on his ass and barks all day!'*

These 'Tales' have been set in Bahrein. In later years our staging post was switched to RAF Masirah.

8
A Tale of Darkness

So we shift from Muharraq eastwards to Masirah Island—that is out of the Persian Gulf to the southern shore of the Gulf of Oman. Now I have described already the imperfections of these desert locations—Aden with its barrenness and scorching heat; Bahrein with its contiguity of squalor and wealth—but they had nothing on Masirah! Masirah had zilch. Rock, desert, heat, yes—but virtually no civilization. There was a nearby settlement known as 'Oil Drum City', because oil drums were the major building material. So, at Masirah the RAF personnel were totally thrown back on their own resources. When one reflects on those days of unaccompanied tours, as this one was, Gan always springs to mind because of its isolated and distant location. Yet compared with the people at Masirah, they were in paradise. It was impossible to make anything of Masirah—it was just a dump. Nevertheless it had spirit as I well know. I spent a long spell there having three engines and an undercarriage leg changed—a later 'Tale'.

Humour shone through. A newcomer entering the Officer's Mess would be surprised to see a door marked 'TV Room'. If curiosity overcame him and he opened it—he would be faced with the desert. It was an outside door labelled by a wit!

Those of you who follow international nature events may well know that Masirah is a place where turtles compulsively come ashore to lay their eggs. Going to see this one night, with the necessary walk along the dark beach, gave me the unique experience of kissing a camel, who had also, obviously, come to the beach to witness the phenomena and accidentally came upon my lips in the night!

This story is concerned with darkness—initially with the lack of it. It was the sad lot of crews, who brought one aircraft in, and then 'rested' to

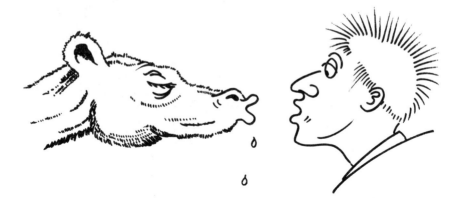

take the next one out, that they had to attempt to sleep in the daytime. This presented all sorts of problems, but the only one I will concentrate on, for the sake of your continued attention, is the thickness of the curtains!

If you are trying to sleep in the middle of a blazing day, then it does not help if the curtains are of similar substance of a dress where you notice, in the sunlight, that the wearer should be wearing an underslip!

The crews passing through, politely suggested that something be done about this! The solution sums up the time and the situation.

One day a 'local' appeared with a pot of paint and painted the glass of the sleeping accommodation windows black! Now there could be no complaints! It was dark! It was like being in the worst sort of prison—which included sharing a cell, for the rooms held eight people (with only a token gesture to privacy, by the arrangement of the furniture). It was dark in those rooms—and they were your 'home' for some days on the 'Changi Slip'.

The scene is now set—The Darkened Room—but now, The Characters. Captain Couth is a quiet, serious minded person, with no time for the 'frivolity' of route life. A measure of this is a particular afternoon, where, with no sense of occasion, he chooses to go to bed in the 'darkened room'. This is partly induced by his desire to isolate himself from the 'rat bags', his navigator and co-pilot who, perhaps, again with no sense of occasion, decide to spend the lunchtime in the bar.

You now have 'The Scene'—'The Darkened Room'—and 'The Characters'. The navigator and co-pilot, whose personal qualities at this point of the story leave something to be desired, return to the communal room, with much play on keeping the noise down and other well intentioned

resolves of the inebriated, which are a total failure. Captain Couth is determined to ignore all this, in his bed in the dark. 'They will calm down in a while'. And they do, Co and Nav, with much accidental noise, do eventually settle on their beds to slip away into their 'six-pints-at-lunchtime' afternoon siesta.

The only noise is the purr, nay roar, of the air conditioner, but that was something you came to accept as normal in those climes. But, after a short while, there is a stir—and a 'stage whisper' from the Nav, '*The trouble with these rooms is that if you want a pee, you have to walk miles to the loo.*' '*Got a problem there, Nav*', murmers the Co. The Captain silently stirs, and buries his head under the pillow. There is silence, but the air is electric with the anticipated problem of the navigator's bladder! A solution is at hand, which is announced, in another stage whisper, by the Nav, '*They've got those metal waste bins in here—I'll use one of those.*'

In the dark could be heard the unmistakable sound of a jet of water impinging on a metal surface! This was too much for our tolerant Captain. Leaping out of his feigned sleep, with one sweep of the hand, he put all the lights on—to reveal, Fred, the Nav, standing there with a jug of water poised over the metal bin!

There are some cruel people in this world. And still more 'Tales'

9
On Our Last Legs

The main relief felt climbing away from the airfield at Masirah was to get away from the heat, the discomfort of which has been heightened by the preparations for departure. There was also the relish that we were on the last part of our journey—home was in sight. But this penultimate leg to Cyprus was a tortuous one. The only political route available to us was North and then West followed by South, over Iran and Turkey. Special diplomatic clearance was need for each flight and the duration of the permission from Turkey was particularly limiting. If we were more than an hour late then clearance had to be renegotiated. This could be one of the difficulties of the route. It was very mountainous and the turbulence could be quite alarming. It was the closest that we ever flew to the 'Iron Curtain'. Looking out of the window was a reminder of the vast areas of the world that are bleak and barren—or covered with water. Some histories have this arid area once water-covered. It is chronicled that it was the site of Noah's Ark.

So relief at leaving the Persian Gulf is temporarily suspended as we plough our way over this uninviting landscape. Then our spirits are restored as we leave the Turkish coast behind us and the island of Cyprus is ahead.

The Britannia knew the island well. Coming into service as the Republic of Cyprus was established, it was consistently called upon, in the country's early turbulent years, to fly in troops as trouble flared up. The establishment of the Republic created the Sovereign Base Areas and the one at Akrotiri held the largest and busiest Station in the Royal Air Force of the 1960s. There was a constant need for supply and the Britannias played their full part. Trooping flights were flown in on a scheduled basis. Many exercises were carried out. Finally the airfield was used, as we are

using it now, as a staging post for flights to the Far East. All this added up to Cyprus being a very familiar place to Britannia crews and a favourite destination. The climate and atmosphere of the island was heightened by our good fortune in being well accommodated.

It did seem that we were witnessing the early days of the Republic establishing itself in the tourist industry. Hotels were slowly being built but the holidaymakers were not yet attracted and the grand new buildings stood largely empty. Whether or not it was a way of helping out, or perhaps the most economical means of accommodating us—whatever the reason, we stayed in hotels in the local town of Limmasol and very pleasant it was too. I remember a particular occasion when our comfort was highlighted. Pushing out the edges of Limmasol, another new hotel had been built on the water's edge. The crew had assembled for breakfast, the patio doors to the beach were partly open, a gentle breeze wafted the long light net curtains and the early morning Mediterranean sun shone warmly. In came a Group Captain Doctor obviously on some medical

hygiene inspection to check on the catering that the crews were having to endure. The look on his face said it all—we never did have it so good!

There was much local colour to enjoy. Life seemed to be lived on the pavements. Old men sat on wicker chairs playing backgammon, drinking coffee the consistency of mud with a glass of water to wash it down. The old ladies wore black. I have this vivid picture of such a lady who had obviously had a difference of opinion with a bus driver who had tossed her and her two chickens, with their legs trussed together, off the bus. She would have come down from the mountains for the market. This was quite a sight in the citrus fruit season. But one needed a strong stomach to tackle the meat market, for another picture I have is of a stall holder carrying in one of those long-eared goats over his shoulder. It was clearly identifiable. All that was missing was its outer skin and hair!

We extended our absorption of the culture to include studies of the night life. In Hero's Square were all the 'night clubs'. I use the term loosely for they bore no relation to the normal concept of such establishments.

These were fairly primitive, natural places—full of boisterous fun. Many were in the open air. This was particularly suitable for one well known act—the Lady on the White Horse. Round and round she rode, bareback. It must have been warm work because she gradually had to take her clothes off. The horse kept its eyes to the front—and so did we!

It was at one of these institutions that my body encountered a unique sensation (!) and that was to experience, at the same time, positive and negative G. The act was roller skaters on a small circular stage. The man had whirled around in the centre with the two girls flying out from his hands performing all manner of manoeuvres. Now he stood down and the

two girls took the centre of the stage, joined hands and spun round and round. A volunteer was sought from the audience—I was thrust forward by my crew. I was then laid across the joined hands and the gyration started. Round and round whizzed my body, its blood trying to escape from the soles of my feet and the top of my head. A unique sensation indeed!

Cyprus is not an entirely happy place with its undercurrent of hostility between the Greeks and the Turks. This led to the establishment of the United Nations peace keeping force and to many troop reinforcements as trouble flared up. This reached such a peak in 1972, that the evacuation of Service families was started and this escalated into the Royal Air Force flying back any UK holidaymaker or resident that wanted to leave. The

Britannias played a major role in this. There were two special flights arranged at the time. One was the 'Stork Special' on which flew all the pregnant wives, in the care of a special team of doctors and midwives.

The second was a 'Pets' Special' and on this were loaded all the cats, dogs and birds that had become the fond possessions of the Service families. There were a considerable number of caged birds. This raised a question, to which theorists might now like to provide the definitive answer. If, as this aircraft was rolling down the runway, the Air Loadmaster had gone down the length of the aircraft rattling all the cages and making the birds fly, would this have reduced the weight of the aircraft?

This evacuation did get quite desperate. Crews went out with their own sheets, food and drink and toilet paper(!) etc, as the facilities were completely overwhelmed. One night I slept in the open air and for the one and only time in my military career heard the sound of hostile gunfire.

Holidaymakers were being lifted by helicopters off the beaches and brought straight to the aircraft, scantily clothed and minus their possessions.

It was one of these civilians who obviously did not understand our military way of doing things that nearly caused one Captain to have apoplexy. Captains of transport aircraft were required, by order, to visit the passenger cabin during the flight to see that all was well—wearing their hats incidentally—again by order. Captain Dave was proceeding, with his accustomed dignity, down the cabin as the passengers were eating, with a smile and a nod and the occasional enquiry as to whether all was well. To his mortification one of the responses he received was, '*Can I have some more butter?*'

All good things must come to an end and the time has come to set course for the last leg home; not that there was any real reluctance. It was probably planned that we would be away for ten days and because of delays this more than likely has stretched to a fortnight, even three weeks. Communication with home has been impossible and as one cruised North it was natural to reflect what had happened whilst one had been away. One thing for sure—you were going to hear it all as soon as you got home.

One day I was waiting in the Passenger Terminal for my wife, Valerie, to pick me up after a particularly lengthy time away. In the distance I could see her approaching in my eight week old, shiny white Renault 16, of which I was particularly proud. I gathered my things and made my way to where she would park. Park she did and rushed towards me(!). '*Don't look at the car! Don't look at the car!*' I look—front wing crumpled. '*What happened there then?*' say I. '*It was an elephant*' was the reply. '*Oh yeah—well I love you. Get in and you can tell me the real story on the way home!*'

But it was an elephant! My wife had taken my sister and her children to the Safari Park at Longleat and an adolescent elephant suddenly decided that it did not like white Renault 16s.

So home at last—a couple of days off—route stand down—and into the Squadron to see what plans have been made for you whilst you have been away. And what are they—your delayed return has narrowed the gap and you are off on another Changi Slip in five days time!

10
Very Important Persons

The Britannias did their share of VIP Flights. With the global nature of our defence commitment, some of these were quite extensive. Her Majesty The Queen only flew once in one of our aircraft and that was only a short flight to Amsterdam.

I only flew VIP's by chance. One day we reported to Akrotiri Operations for what was only anticipated as a straightfoward run back to Lyneham. Fairly casually it was mentioned that there was a particular Major on board—HRH The Duke of Kent! But he was travelling in his Army role and wanted to be treated like a normal passenger. Well even we mere 'run of the mill' squadron crew could do that! All was going well until we started getting very dismal forecasts of the weather at Lyneham and a diverson seemed inevitable.

I felt compelled to break away from 'the normal passenger' constraint and advise HRH of this and ask if there were any messages we could send. 'No, Thank you.' He was quite content to allow things to take their course. On return to the flight deck, I reported events to the crew on the intercomm. Now this means of communication has a brotherhood. There is a secrecy about it and things are said that would not be for other ears—in this case Royal ones!

It happens so many times that gloomy weather forecasts are not fulfilled and this was going to be the case. As we descended and turned over Swindon, Lyneham could be clearly seen in the distance. At that very moment, before perhaps making some remark brought about by the welcome sight, I glanced over my shoulder to see the Duke standing on the flight deck WITH A HEADSET ON! The AQM, without a word to anyone, had decided that it would be good idea for him to see and hear what was going on! How close we had come to causing Royal offence!

A story is told of a similar situation where the VIP is the Commander-in-Chief and he too is standing on the flight deck, with a headset on, but with the full knowledge of the crew. The AQM appears, adjusts his microphone to his lips and leans towards the Captain and says in a low voice, but for all on intercomm to hear, '*I think that the C-in-C's a bit of a Charlie*', or words to that effect (?)! The poor Captain is nearly passing out. Then he is quietly shown the plug of the C-in-C's headset, which the AQM had temporarily disconnected from the system!

The theme of VIP allows the introduction of a real old 'folk tale'. A Royal Air Force Comet VIP crew had the task, back in the 1960s, of taking the then Foreign Secretary to Moscow. A Western military aircraft movement behind the Iron Curtain was a rare event and was accompanied by much caution and suspicion. Russian aircrew members had to be picked up at an airfield before entering Soviet airspace.

There was an exceptional feature to this particular flight in that the aircraft and crew remained in Moscow whilst the Foreign Secretary went about his business. It was more usual for the crew to drop their passengers and retire to the haven of a Scandinavian country to await for a return across the border, when the pick-up was required. So the crew found themselves in a Moscow hotel for a few days. Now it is not an unknown feature of aircrew route life that having arrived in the hotel, the mecca is one of the member's bedroom to talk over the flight—and of other things—and perhaps consume the odd alcoholic beverage!

On this occasion the conversation inevitaby turned to the unusual security situation in which they found themselves and from this stemmed

the thought that the room they were in was possibly bugged. The suggestion was made that they should search the room. There was initial disappointment—wardrobes were inspected, light fittings scrutinized, tables and chairs examined, pictures turned over—all to no avail. '*What about under the bed?*'

Eagerly the bed was moved and sure enough, under the carpet was an ominous lump. The carpet was rolled back and the crew's mistrust was confirmed. Revealed to them was a suspicious looking metal cap. Now many flight engineers of those days carried quite a comprehensive tool kit—plus a variety of fuses, nuts and bolts, seals etc which they gradually collected and now carried like talismen against gremlins striking their aircraft. The engineer was despatched to fetch his tool kit.

The cap had a nut-like shape and he did have a spanner to fit it. After some initial resistance he was able to move the cap and anticipation heightened, in wonder at what would be revealed beneath it. Suddenly the cap came loose and, simultaneously, the sound of an enormous crash from the floor below reached their ears. Sheepishly they investigated and found a huge chandelier lying in a thousand pieces on the floor of the deserted ballroom below!

11
Tales of Oil

The year 1966 was a busy time for the Britannia fleet. On top of all the normal commitments, there was a job to be done in Africa.

Towards the end of 1965 the Ian Smith Government of Rhodesia made its Unilateral Declaration of Independence (UDI) and, as a result, sanctions were imposed by Britain. This placed Zambia, to the north, in a difficult position as all its communications were through its southern neighbour. Consequently, we gave considerable economic aid to Zambia, including an airlift of essential oil supplies. That airlift was provided by the RAF Britannias and was to continue for the best part of 1966, the rate of supply building up to 100 tons a day.

Picture, if you will, this commercial airliner that the Royal Air Force had bought as a strategic transport aircraft, in the role of a flying fuel lorry. Admittedly it had a strengthened floor and a freight door. But the sill of this door was more than ten feet from the ground. It was hardly tailor-made for the carriage of oil.

Lyneham was always a barometer of world affairs and the first signs of the impending problem in Southern Africa was a series of flights and stand-bys in the December of '65 when a Javelin detachment was being positioned at Lusaka for the air defence of Zambia. The frustration of the Britannia crews on the initial stand-by, in Nairobi, can be judged from them forming themselves into 'The Mushroom Club'. They felt that they were being kept in the dark and fed on horse shit! The mushroom remained the symbol of this operation. In charge, at that time, was a Wing Commander Brownlow, whom idle minds renamed 'Brown Commander Winglow'! It did all seem a false alarm, for, as Christmas approached we were all recovered to Lyneham. But the situation obviously grew more tense as Christmas drew even nearer. Britannias, along with 100 Britannia souls, were despatched to spend the festive season at Dar-es-Salaam, Tanzania, poised to fly to Zambia.

The renamed and reborn Tanganyika was flexing its muscles under its new found position. Part of this was the creation of status symbols, and one of these was the brand new, five star Hotel Kilimanjaro. Their first customers were the Britannia Detachment! I think we did each other a mutual good turn. They were certainly practising—we, most assuredly, were in the most superior route accommodation that we had ever experienced. The senior staff were European and they had to keep a close eye on their African trainees. The chambermaids wore a stylized version of the local dress! This must have been replaced after a while on the grounds of practicality. Being draped in several yards of colourful material may have looked quite striking but it did rather hinder bed making!

One wonders who the Hotel's customers would have been in the downstairs Night Club, had we not been there, But there was no time for the management to contemplate—we were there!

Flying down to Zambia began in earnest and some crews flew on Christmas Day. They entered the flight in red in their log books!

We became accustomed to being 'extras' in this national showpiece. As we sat in the Hotel, there would be a continual stream of local sightseers, encouraged to see this symbol of their country's new standing. There was to be a grander 'showing off' on New Year's Eve. The local dignitaries were invited to 'our' night club! We were asked if we would not use the Club that night, but the management laid on a bar and buffet for us to see the New Year in by the swimming pool.

Now this was something of an error—water does take on magnetic properties as an evening progresses! The first aquatic move was made by a crew who thought it a little dull sitting by the poolside and took their table and chairs into the shallow end and sat down! Before long a full scale swimming gala was in progress. One diver had to put in an extra 'half pike' or whatever at the last minute of his dive to avoid a plate of sandwiches floating on the water! Nobody noticed the Press photographer but in the next day's paper, under the headline 'The RAF Plays It Cool', was a picture of a couple, fully clothed, dancing waist deep in water!

The very efficient, immaculately turned out, Swiss Maitre d'Hotel came to see that all was well as the bewitching hour approached. The temptation was too much and there was a move to throw him in the pool. But he was not a smooth hotel manager for nothing. In his polite but firm way he persuaded the unruly to do no such thing—but he would send the under manager along! And he did—and in the pool the subordinate went!

It was intended that we should take a full floor load of 50 gallon oil drums twice a day in each of the five aircraft to Zambia. There was obviously some nervousness on the part of Tanzania about this, signalled by us being ordered to fly in civilian clothes. This heralded the end of Dar-es-Salaam as our springboard to Zambia and in a few days the detachment was moved to Nairobi from where the operation, which became known as the 'Oil Lift', was to continue until October.

The two Zambian airfields, one at the capital Lusaka the other by the northern town of Ndola, were high with short runways. Sufficient crews were detached so that each crew did one run a day. If you were on the morning run, which started very early, the afternoon run seemed more attractive. But when you were back in time for that lunch-time beer you were glad that the day's work was done.

With that freight door sill over ten feet above the ground, the Britannia did not lend itself to the loading of oil drums. And when loaded they were not the easiest things to secure with chains to floor points. But a slick procedure soon became established. Perhaps this is best illustrated by the unloading process that developed. Fork lift trucks are not the friends of aircraft. It is almost inevitable that if you manoeuvre one often enough up to an aircraft then at some stage a fork is going to pierce the aircraft skin. We were also in a hurry, another ingredient for an accident. The solution was to keep the fork lift truck stationary. It was positioned below the freight door, the forks raised to the sill and two barrels rolled on. The forks were then lowered and, just above the ground, they were tilted forwards and off rolled the barrels. Waiting 'local lads' were ready to take advantage of the momentum and roll the barrels away from the aircraft. The forks were then tilted back and up to the door they went again. With this system, and time saved by starting the unlashing of the load as the aircraft taxied in, the turn around time was fined down to twenty minutes.

But not everything was so slick and efficient. The first Britannia to land on the Oil Lift was given a grand welcome. President Kaunda was at the airport to greet the crew. The photograph that appeared in the newspapers did not convey what should have been the dignity of the occasion. It showed the President underneath the aircraft peering at the undercarriage, the wheels of which had sunk a foot into the tarmac of the taxyway. We learnt not to cut corners after that. Mind you we were not the only ones with such problems. Our Javelins, on air defence stand-by there, had to fly every day and not return to the same dispersal spot otherwise they, too, had that sinking feeling!

All the mistakes were not made at our humble level. There were an awful lot of misunderstandings by our commanders. A fairly senior officer discovered one day that we were speaking to the Rhodesian Air Traffic Control services en route. This was a natural and sensible thing to do as we were flying for part of the route in their airspace. '*Don't do it*', exploded the Senior Officer.

However, after some explanation he saw the necessity of our communication which then produced the order, 'Well, speak to them abruptly, then.'

It was a ludicrous situation. BOAC was still operating their VC10 service through Lusaka to Salisbury, Rhodesia and picking up fuel in Lusaka to do it!

Regular operations do produce efficient methods but they also result in some complacency. I set off one morning on the dawn run south westward and at the top of climb the silence, induced by our early rising, was broken with someone enquiring whether our load was for Lusaka or Ndola. No one knew. The paperwork for the flight did not help—and the oil barrels were totally uncommunicative. So we guessed Lusaka. If we were wrong, no one told us.

The aforementioned problem of the ten foot gulf between the ground and the aircraft floor had long presented a challenge in the efficient and speedy loading and unloading of the aircraft. In the early days a device had been built and it was known as the Britannia Freight Lift Platform (BFLP)—and many other names! It was a 10ft × 10ft platform, with a lifting framework, that was placed on the ground, below the freight door. It was then loaded and raised to the height of the aircraft cargo floor. The power to raise the platform could be obtained by running No 3 engine. But it was a fickle thing. One was positioned at Lusaka. One day I was told that we were to be in the aeromedical role out of Lusaka. Our patient was a very ill, retired senior Zambian Army officer, obviously one who was a legacy from the colonial days. He was being flown back to England.

Off came the oil barrels and the aircraft was prepared for its hospital role—and the dreaded BFLP was positioned at the freight door. The ambulance appeared with the stretchered patient and the Band of the Zambian Army. The stretcher and its attendants mounted the platform which then started its slow agonising ascent. The band played a solemn farewell. After rising a foot the platform stopped. With much poking and twiddling there were signs of life and with squeaks and groans the rise continued, albeit very slowly. The band reached the end of its piece, in spite of having repeated many of the passages a number of times. In the silence the agonising noises of the lift seemed to fill the air. The band started up again. After what seemed an age the door sill was reached. What an embarrassment for our modern air transport force.

While we flew daily, progress was being made on a road link to enable Zambia to be supplied other than through its southern neighbour and in October, with it complete, it was time for the Britannias to withdraw. I flew the last aircraft out of Nairobi for the UK at a specially authorized high weight known as Military Operating Standard (MOS) weight. It was loaded, with the Detachment equipment, in a day-long downpour and I swear it was 10,000 lbs overweight, twice the extra allowed by MOS. It took us half an hour to climb overhead Nairobi before we had sufficient height to safely set course.

So ended a chapter in the history of the RAF Britannias. Of what consequence is it now?

12
A Tale of Bother

A feature of Royal Air Force aircrew life is that if you fly a particular aircraft for a long time you are considered to be good at it. It may well be that you are actually quite skilled or it could be that the people who are now in a position to judge you as 'good' are your contemporaries or even 'junior' to you on the aircraft type and other factors influence them.

For whatever reason, I did become to be considered 'good' enough on the Britannia to become an instructor on the Operational Conversion Unit (OCU). The term 'instructor' was something of an anomaly in the early days of the transport world as the training staff spent more time examining than instructing. The former definitely overshadowed the latter. Examiners, or 'trappers' as they were known when language was restrained—there were other coarser terms—were the bane of the 1960s transport pilot's life. Things improved over the years (and I hope I was part of that betterment) but when I started, a periodic local flying test, the day/night cat or a route check struck terror in our hearts. They were conducted by unreal people. They did not seem to have any human past. It seemed as though they had been born 'trappers'.

One's introduction to them was on the conversion course for the aircraft. To use the word 'course' is something of a misnomer as it implies some form of instruction. This was almost entirely lacking though it has to be admitted that if, on your first flight, you showed signs that you were never going to be able to strap yourself into the seat, adjust it or sort your headset out and thus jeopardize the sortie ever getting airborne, there would be some begrudging advice as to what to do. But that would be it. The approach from then on was, 'I can do it—and I'm pretty good—I have no way or real wish to convey to you how it is done—you will just have to pick up what you can.' So you had your pitiful go. Then the teaching strategy became clear. You were left in no doubt that what you had done was wrong but any guidance as to how to do it right was kept a closely guarded secret.

And so we stumbled on and eventually were warily considered just acceptable to be allowed to join the Squadron. Any relief at having escaped the attentions of those oppressors was short-lived for now you met them in their examiner role. Out of the blue they would appear along a route somewhere to give you a 'route-check'. During this you were supposed to operate and behave quite normally whilst they observed and made notes for later comment. Imagine it with your job. You have someone sitting there—watching—not motionless. There will be, now and again, a heave and a sigh from him, as you do something, followed by a burst of note taking. But just carry on and work and 'behave quite normally'! But why did we contribute to the perpetuation of this system by caring so much what the outcome of it all was? I suppose the simple answer is 'pride'. There was a grading system 'A', 'B', 'C', 'D' and 'E'. 'A' was exceptional and was a qualification required to fly the Royal Family. 'E' meant you were so dismal a failure that it was considered that you needed further training before you could safely operate again. It is my record that I did, over the years, collect the 'full house'!

More enlightened times did come to pass and 'training' was introduced as an essential part of the categorization procedure. Instead of the 'instant death' day/night cat, a fortnight of refresher training would be carried out with an OCU instructor and his opinion of your performance, at the end, determined your grade. Similarly, an instructional aspect was introduced into the route check. It was, at the introduction of these more civilized ways, that I joined the OCU. There was a strange aspect to this recruitment in that you went through the 'old' system—route check, day/night cat, simulator, ground exams—by a 'trapper' of 'trappers'!

With the memories of my own initiation into Britannia flying still vivid, I was determined to be more humane, trying to create a more relaxed atmosphere in which people might learn. Something of my style may be gleaned from samples of my oral ground examination. 'What is the longest continuous piece of metal in the aircraft—and I'll tell you it's not the main spar because that's got joints in it?' Much thought— 'Wing panels?' 'No,' 'Flooring?' 'No.' 'Engine main shaft?' 'No,' 'Give in'—'The windings of the alternator!'

We had 23 Britannias, 20 designated Mk Is and 3 Mk 2s, determined, essentially, by differences in the passenger/cargo compartment. Question: 'You are standing outside a Britannia. How can you tell whether it's a

Mk I or a Mk 2?' Much puzzling—thoughts about toilet and galley drains seem fruitful. 'No—there is a much more obvious way.' No, still this hang-up about effluents. 'Well, look at the tail, check the number—the Mk 2s are 404, 392 and 398!'

I enjoyed my spell on the OCU. There were tedious times back at base but we had a fairly free choice of routes that we route checked AND instructed on. We took each course on a full global circumnavigation trainer and we had our own route flights 'to keep our hand in'. There were also 'one-off' flights and it was relating the tale of one such of these that was my original intent.

Whether it was in the mind or was a fact, it did appear that the performance of the Britannia was deteriorating as the years rolled by. Alongside dull evidence of increased 'times to height' and cruising speeds below the targets proclaimed by the performance manuals, would be set vivid tales, from 'tired and emotional' crews, of 'hairy' take-offs. Whether you were influenced by one or the other (or both) there was a general discomfort.

Then, one hot, sultry day at the airport of Mombasa, on the coast of Kenya, a Britannia started its take-off run down a fairly critical runway lengthwise given the take-off factors of temperature, wind, height and weight. All these had, routinely, been considered before departure as part of the pre-flight planning and all, in theory, was well for the necessary weight at take-off. Full power was set, with the added amount given by 'water injection'. The engines looked good, brakes off and the aircraft started its trundle down the runway. Trundle is an apt word, for the Britannia was always particularly slow to accelerate in these tropical conditions. It was not unusual, therefore, for the level of anxiety on the flight deck to rise as the runway length was gradually being eaten up. It was unusual, indeed unheard of, for events to progress as they did. The Captain began to express doubts about the aircraft being able to get airborne in the amount of runway remaining. The pitch of his voice rose as that doubt increased. And that uncertainty reached the point that he decided to abandon the take-off. What had happened was a first because never before had a Britannia Captain had sufficient doubt of his calculated take-off performance to take this dramatic step.

Now here was a puzzle. The weather conditions that would affect the take-off agreed with those forecast and on which the calculation had been based. Was the aircraft heavier than stated? Off came all the freight and it was check-weighed. The recalculation agreed with the first. This only left mechanical fault—were the brakes binding? They would have to be checked. The problem was now taking on great proportions—and it was only a few days before Christmas—and amongst those on board were *Pam's People*. Are you old enough to remember them? An aircraft was diverted from the Singapore route to replace the lame one, the load transferred. It took off uneventfully at a weight and in similar conditions to the abandoned take-off.

The technical investigation of the lame duck continued. The brakes were not binding. Were the engines suspect? Were they developing full power? Engine No 1 was started and the routine for ground runs commenced. The target power figure had been determined back at base and was recorded on a placard on the flight deck. The throttle was slowly advanced and the power check parameters set—but the engine was 'down'! The torque developed did not come up to the target figure. So the problem had been isolated. But wait—No 2 engine was tested—'down'! No 3—'down'—and you've already guessed that No 4 followed suit. By standards normally applied, all four engines were unserviceable. I will not dwell on this Mombasa situation any longer. It was decided in the end that all four engines could not be suspect. There must be something wrong with the run-up procedures in hot and humid conditions. So, with the aircraft now empty and with minimum fuel, it was decided all would be well. The aircraft took off safely and returned to the UK.

Back at Brize Norton the engines were tested. They were all normal and on target! So now there is a problem.

Out of all this came a decision to arrange a special flight to check aircraft performance and to examine engine running techniques in the tropics. A well worn route was chosen—one with which you are now familiar—to Singapore and return. The flying performance of the aircraft was to be checked by measuring the height to which it climbed in the configuration it would be in if an engine failed on the runway at too high a speed for the aircraft to be stopped in the remaining length. The 'decision speed' is calculated for each take-off—below it the aircraft is stopped, if an engine fails—above it the take-off continues, the engine is shut down and the propeller feathered and the undercarriage retracted. The aircraft is climbed at a calculated speed which ensures maximum terrain clearance. All this can be calculated and is done if the take-off path is over rising ground and the aircraft weight is high. Because the graphs are available to do this, it is a useful datum to assess aircraft performance.

I was nominated aircraft captain for this trip which promised to be different—but the difference went beyond that anticipated. The route was to be Brize Norton to Akrotiri, Cyprus and then, instead of our normal staging post of Masirah, we were to use the recently constructed Seeb International on the North East coast of Muscat and Oman. Gan was the next stop then on to Singapore, where we were now using Tengah. It was then about turn for the reverse route.

Our instructions were that, after take-off at all these places, we were to set ourselves up with our No 4 engine shut down, propeller feathered, undercarriage up, flaps at 15 degrees and then climb with full power for five minutes and record the height gain achieved. This would then be compared with a figure obtained from the appropriate performance graph. On the ground the two technicians we had on board—having, incidentally, true Service names: Chalky White and Spud Murphy—were to carry out engine ground runs using post-Mombasa parameters.

So off from Brize Norton we set—a motley crew. The Co-pilot was Flying Officer Dick King, on his first operational flying tour and, like so many of his ilk, a sharp, sensible and extremely competent young man. The Navigator could give him a year or two! Flight Lieutenant 'Rev' Wilkins, very experienced and an OCU instructor. Master Engineer Paddy Tranter was the Air Engineer, again a wise old hand with many years of flying experience. Down the back were two equally 'hairy' ALMs, Paddy Harper and Sam Justin. Out of place in this crew was a young WRAF Sergeant, Janet Robinson. She was awaiting her ALM Course and had been put on the flight for 'experience'!

We proceeded to Cyprus and braced ourselves for the first of our unusual departures. Airborne from Akrotiri, heading out to sea, 1,000 feet, shut down No 4, check undercarriage up, 15 degrees flap set. Ready? Full power, climbing and timing. Five minutes later we were at 5,000 feet—with sighs of relief. We were not used to such goings-on!

Now we were back to normal and proceeding to Seeb. This was one of a number of new airports being built to international standards by the rich oil states. But we were not to have long to wonder at it. This was a double-leg day. Akrotiri to Seeb—90 minute refuel—Seeb to Gan. We had arrived at Seeb in the cool of the evening—a mere 30°C. Refuelling proceeded, flight planning calculations complete, time to go.

We were heavy—it was hot—the Britannia was in 'trundle' mode, but the new runway was good and long and after what seemed an age we clawed our way into the pitch black desert sky. Not for us the settling down into the normal route flying routine. There was our performance check to do.

It seemed a foolish thing to be doing, shutting an engine down in this hot and hostile environment, but that was our job and these were just the conditions for which figures were needed. So once again 5, 4—full power—3, 2, I go! The Britannia wallowed upwards with the three engines gulping the hot night air. The rate of climb was poor—time seemed to stand still. Four of the five planned minutes had elapsed, the flight deck had a somewhat anxious air. Then there was what seemed like an explosion of lights—red ones!

On each of the pilot's instrument panels was a central red light which indicated that there was a fault on the electrical panel located, rather obscurely, behind the co-pilot's seat. These two lights were ON! Eyes sped to the electrical panel—three red lights ON! And, what is more they indicated the most serious fault that could occur on that panel—alternator overheat—(or should it be alternator overheats?). Three lights showed Nos 1, 2 and 3 alternators overheating. The only reason for No 4 not being on was, remember, that No 4 engine was shut down!

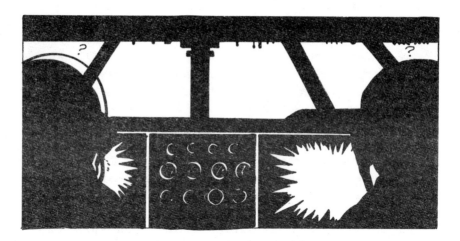

The alternators of the Britannia were permanently connected to the engine so the only way of stopping them was to stop the engine. The drill then for an overheating alternator was to shut down the associated engine—with No 4 already shut down, at least things would be symmetrical!

Clearly something less drastic had to be done. Power was reduced to a minimum and Paddy qualified for an entry into the *Guinness Book of Records* for the quickest engine relight drill ever carried out—No 4 was up and running and giving valuable full power. With the lower power setting, No 1 overheat had cancelled so that throttle was advanced to allow Nos 2 and 3 to be completely closed. This had half the desired effect—No 2 light went out. No 3 persisted so that engine was shut down and feathered. All this took place very quickly—perhaps only slightly longer than it has taken you to read about it!

While the Engineer's hands had been rippling over the switches, buttons and throttles, the Navigator had determined the best way to turn for Seeb for maximum terrain clearance and the co-pilot declared our emergency on the radios. It is not recorded what the Loadmasters were doing!

But now a relative calm had returned. Albeit that we had one engine shut-down, the aircraft was flying safely and the fault with the alternators unlikely to return—unless we were foolish enough to try full power for five minutes at low speed again! In this situation, Seeb did not seem a sensible place to go with Masirah just down the road with all its servicing facilities. So, to Masirah we headed. A lot of beer was consumed that night in the specially opened Sergeants' Mess Bar. Perhaps that is really why landing at Seeb did not seem a good idea!

The ground engineers were examining the aircraft. The alternators did not look too bad but they were changed so that they could be examined in the UK. The heat sensing devices which were linked to the overheat warning lights were also changed. The aircraft was declared serviceable and we were cleared to go. But our instructions were to proceed normally. No more performance testing for the time being!

So we settled to a gentle, normal route flight to Singapore. By the time we arrived there the matter had been considered by our masters and it had been decided that we could resume the trial at Gan—in fact we were to stay at Gan for several days and fly special flights out of there. All went well—no overheats. We, as a crew, became overheated one day. We were getting tired and we had just done our fourth or fifth trip, climbing on three engines, trying not to stare at the overheat warning lights. We were asked if, on our return to Gan, we would simulate an emergency situation for the Fire Service and, after landing, turn off the runway and shut-down. The emergency vehicles would then surround us and do their bit. I reluctantly agreed on condition that the fatigued crew would not be involved.

We duly landed and turned into the loop at the end of the runway, a piece of concrete, by the way, so close to the water's edge you felt you could reach out of the window and dapple your hand in the turquoise water. We did join in a bit by deploying one of our escape chutes, down which the crew slid. This was somewhat devious though—we thought we would get to the bar quicker that way! At the bottom we were greeted by the Warrant Officer Fire Chief, '*The aircrew resuscitation equipment is on the back of the Land Rover, Sir.*' I inwardly groaned, my message about our non-involvement had obviously not got through. But it would have been wrong to argue so we meekly trooped to our fate at the Land Rover—to be greeted by a case of cold beer!

From Gan we continued home. There we were quizzed on our 'goings-on' and awaited the decision of where we were to go from there. The answer came a month later—we were to go to Singapore and back, repeating the trial. An additional feature was the fitting of heat-sensitive strips to the alternator ducting to investigate the temperatures therein. This was to be the start of more trouble!

13
Can the Bother Be Repeated?

With the benefit of two months' healing of the memory wound left by all those red lights, we set off once again with our own aircraft to Singapore. With us came an engineering officer whose particular concern, being in charge of Brize Norton's Electrical Section, was the validity of the warnings that we had previously received. With no signs of damage to the alternators, the integrity of the overheat warning system was put in doubt.

Our plan therefore was to repeat the 'second segment' climbs at each staging post. Whilst the aircraft was on the ground heat sensitive strips in various parts of the alternator ducting would be removed, examined and renewed. So we would be building up additional performance data and information on the alternators' temperature behaviour in these adverse conditions of low speed at high power in hot climes.

Lest it be thought that we were allowed to take our time about all this, it is interesting to note that my log book records that we flew Brize Norton, Malta, Cyprus, Masirah, Karachi, Gan, Colombo, Singapore, Colombo, Gan, Karachi, Masirah in eight days! But we were to have an enforced rest at that last stop.

On the morning of 20 July 1973, Masirah was its normal unexciting self—hot, in spite of a steady breeze. Britannia XL635 was being prepared for our departure. This included filling the engines' water tanks with demineralized water. We were to use 'water injection' for take off which would give us the extra engine power necessary at our weight and the airfield temperature.

Six sticky crew members climbed on board the aircraft at eight o'clock and started the preparations. The Engineering Officer reported that the temperature recorders had been renewed. At ten to nine we were on the runway ready to go. There was always a slight anxiety about a 'wet' take-off in the Britannia. One did not know whether the water was actually going to flow until full power had been applied. Today we were OK—four green lights, water flowing, extra power being given by the engines. As we climbed away and began a lazy turn back over the airfield, to set course for Cyprus, many of our cares should have been over. But not for this crew—we were still doing our engine shut-down and five minute climb.

Preparations for this were slick—this was our eleventh in eight days. All is set, No 4 shut down, 15 degrees of flap—just full power to set. Suddenly there is an unmistakeable lurch of the aircraft. All eyes flash to the engine instruments—the lurch is in sequence with the needles associated with No 1 engine. The aircraft swung left in sympathy with those needles rotating anti-clockwise. The sway to the right came as they reversed their rotation. The engine flame was being extinguished and relit just as it would be in those icing conditions which have been described. But the only ice you were likely to experience in the Masirah area, upwards as well as along, for many a mile, was that in your gin and tonic! No, there was something radically wrong with that No 1 engine and the device for ultimate defence against ice—a continually glowing plug in one of the combustion chambers—was the only thing preventing a complete shut-down.

The Flight Engineer, Eddy Godwin, obviously came from the same stable as Paddy Tranter, whose record he equalled for re-starting No 4 engine. This done, No 1 was put out of its spasm by being shut-down. So it was 'Masirah, we're coming back'. Such a return in a large transport aircraft is not entirely straightforward. There is a landing weight restriction and, at take-off and for a number of hours afterwards, until fuel is used up, the aircraft will be above that limit. For this reason a fuel jettison system is standard and we were now to utilize it. This is never done lightly—one always has in mind the potential fireball to be created as fuel is discharged from pipes in the wings and atomizes as it meets the high speed airflow. All was well, check list followed, the necessary amount of fuel had been dumped.

Hindsight would have shaken what complacency we had as we sprayed the desert with our inflammable load. Firstly, the engineer observed that the engine parameters of our relit No 4 engine were not compatible with 2 and 3, a clear indication of some incipient failure. Normal operating procedures called for it to be shut down but with No 1 in that condition already this seemed injudicious and so it was throttled back to the idle position and left there for the rest of the flight.

Next, and of some significance to our only just past 'fireball condition'; when we came to retract the throttles of our only two serviceable engines, the inboards, they displayed the same symptoms as No 1, which had started this whole drama off. They were 'autorelighting'—the business where the flame was going out and being re-ignited by the glow plug. But now we had some 'very aware of predicament' people down at back of the aircraft. AQM Howard Tonks told us that with each 'autorelight' there was a huge tongue of flame from the engine jet pipe as unspent fuel was ignited. What if that had happened during our fuel jettison!

A haze had settled over Masirah during our absence and with one engine shut-down, one throttled back and two only giving intermittent power, we completed a very uneasy radar approach and landed— thankfully! All this must have made us very thirsty because we drank a lot of beer that lunchtime!

The next ten days were unique in Britannia history. It was decided that we needed three of our engines changed and whilst preparations for this were afoot the aircraft was moved to a more convenient location. Whilst it was being manoeuvred a huge casting in the undercarriage cracked—a crack wide enough to to take a fist! Never was a 'Whispering Giant' so sick.

I will never forget the feeling of possible guilt as to whose fault this whole thing was as a Belfast aircraft lumbered in with our three engines and undercarriage leg to be followed by a re-routed VC10 with all the necessary ground crew. They set to work in the boiling sun and to their credit completed the task in just over a week.

It was time for the air test to check their work out and all went remarkably well. At the end of the morning we were able to declare the aircraft serviceable and fit to depart the next day for the UK.

It must have been the relief that caused me, completely out of character(!), to over-indulge that lunch-time—and through the afternoon, with my equally relieved ground and aircrew. As the sun went down, but the party showed no signs of abating, I decided enough was enough and headed towards what was now a well known refuge, the Visiting Aircraft Servicing Flight, for a cup of black coffee.

Although it was well after normal working hours, the place was not deserted and I was greeted by, '*Hello Sir, you're the first—make a cup of coffee and have a seat.*'

In my befuddled condition it took a long time for me to realise what was going on. A bed sheet was being pinned to the wall, cables unwound across the room—the assembly of equipment—with knobs and switches, two circular objects on arms, a glass eye. Ah—a film projector! And the room was now filling up. I had stumbled on my first (and last) blue movie show!

Curiosity overcame the remnants of conscience I had left and as the film rolled, I concentrated. I was reminded of the instructions that went with those incredibly clever and complex plastic aircraft construction kits which were then just establishing themselves. The first directive, always, was to 'identify the parts'. With the bad quality of the film and my disabled vision, I failed to single out any 'parts' and my inquisitiveness about things indecent portrayed on the silver screen remained unassuaged.

Four engined aircraft are safe on the premise that it is virtually impossible for coincident faults to strike all the engines at the same time. The one weak link is the communal fuel and for that reason stringent precautions are taken with its purity. Checks showed the Masirah fuel to be uncontaminated. But subsequent examination of our engines in the UK led to doubts abut the purity of the demineralised water used during the take-off. Valves that are closed then, at full power, have to open, later, at lower power settings to maintain the balance of air to fuel in the engine. The signs were that these could not open, when they should, due to contamination. The water, which came from a special point in Masirah's desalinization plant, was found to be impure. The cause of much anxiety had been found.

14
Westward for a Change

A route flight away from the Changi Slip, the Mediterranean or Germany was a rare treat for the average squadron member of those days. There was a clique, known as the 'Country Club'. who did manage to secure more than their fair share.

One time, however, when grander parts were visited by us lesser brethren, was when the westbound reinforcement of the Far East was excercised. This elaborate operation took place once a year. It was argued that if we were to be seen able to fulfil our defence commitments in the Far East then we must be capable of doing this across the territories of our North American allies rather than via the shorter, but in times of tension, possibly politically tumultuous regions which lay beneath our normal eastbound route.

On the declared day, Exercise 'Travelling Causeway' would start, the first phase being to position the ground crews and the aircraft slip crews at each staging post. The route varied over the years but one of the first was Lyneham, Thule AFB Greenland, Elmendorf AFB Alaska, Midway Island and Guam in the Pacific and then Singapore. With all in position the first exercise aircraft proper would leave Lyneham and the stream would follow at four-hourly intervals, stopping only to refuel and change crews. This grand plan came to an untimely halt on the first run. All the slip crews and ground crew had reached Greenland on the positioning phase when the exercise was cancelled because of the requirement to fly troops from the UK to Aden, the scene of much unrest for many years to come. Back we all trooped to the UK. Another start was made two months later. Six aircraft on the main lift set off at the two hourly intervals from Lyneham. Five of them made it, all that distance to Singapore, within five hours of the schedule.

That sixth aircraft, which developed a propeller fault between Alaska and Midway Island, provided me with a memorable week.

Midway was manned by the US Navy—and 'officer-wife-womanned'. The commissioned lot had their wives—no such luck for the enlisted. If one ignored the military presence, it was a paradise island. White sand, turquoise-blue sea, the assaults of the sun tempered by a gentle breeze. But civilization was there, which provided us with three B's within a 100 yard radius: a Beach, a Bar and a Bed! Another essential ingredient of the almost tourist nature of our stay was the bird-life, represented primarily by the Gooney Birds. We were there at the stage when the chicks—if you could use such a word about something the size of a big duck—were starting to fly. We learnt that the parent Gooney Birds returned to precisely the same spot each year to lay one egg. This was tended by the female whilst the male on his long, thin, glider-like wings, soared many miles from the island in search of food. This was regurgitated on return to feed the chick. As it grew, Mum had to go foraging as well and if the chick moved, or was moved, from its spot in that time, the parents would be unable to find it.

Anyway, it was highly amusing come flying time. We lay in the sun watching the build-up to this. A promising sign was 'engine run-ups'. These huge offspring, with their already large wing span, would stand into wind and exercise their wings, Flap, flap, flap—a bigger flap and a slight lift

into the air. But the next step was a greater one—a run into wind with the wings flapping. This was the one to watch. It would most likely stop and fall over. But there was a chance that it would get airborne—and then it would be flying like a . . . bird (?). All their awkwardness on the ground was transformed into grace in the air. But wait, the ground was still to be contended with on landing. The thing to do was to keep an eye on a particular one of these 'first soloists' and watch out for its attempt to land. It was all there; the unsteady, uncertain approach—and overshoot. Try again—better approach, some nervousness at the end—overshoot. Round again! This time, awful approach, desperate last stage, catastrophic landing—head over heels, a blur of feathers and feet! But down. If you examine a Gooney Bird, it does have a very well developed breast bone that generations of such landings have evolved.

Whilst our aircraft was being fixed (a new propeller had to be flown in first) the days drifted by. We taught the US Navy how to play darts. One afternoon an invitation came for us to go along to one of the Officer's rooms for a 'sundowner'. This stretched our politeness to the maximum as it had been noticed that this particular host had held couple of evening Bible classes during our stay. Feeling that we might be a captive congregation, we politely trooped along to the room. We sat in a mannerly circle. '*I hear you guys like Dry Martinis,*' says the 'God-botherer', producing an enormous bottle of gin, ice and dry martini. Into a jug goes all the gin. '*I make them really dry, only two fingers of dry martini!*' Ice is added—'*and only two stirs*'. The glasses are filled and we sit genteely until everyone has one. '*Here's to you Brits.*' '*Cheers,*' say we and sip. Further conversation was difficult for a while with our cheeks and lips locked against our teeth.

The pain subsided—glasses refilled—no pain at all! The RC Padre popped in and rapidly diminished our lead on the number of glasses. He had been a noticeable character on the beach, sunbathing all day, wearing a rather stylish straw hat. I commented on the hat—he admired my Britannia tie (in true British style we were with tie and long sleeved shirt)—a swap was agreed. I gave him my tie—I never did get the hat. The chances of my conversion to Roman Catholicism had been slight before all this—now they were reduced to zero.

Long stops like this tend to heighten any tensions in a crew and some outspokenness can occur. I was the humble co-pilot and I don't think the Captain was too impressed with my sociability. Perhaps my feelings about him showed. The outcome of this, one evening, was the statement that, when we did get going, I would do everything as if I was the Captain—'that should teach me!' When we eventually set off it was a very glum and silent occupant of the left-hand seat. And he sat there and sat there. Eventually I had to break the 'sound' barrier and say that I needed to go down the back for natural reasons. *'You'll have to wait—I'm dying to go myself—but I was waiting for you to say I could!'* There were some funny, obtuse, over-inflated Captains around in those days.

Later routings of 'Travelling Causeway' and other flights took us more often into the United States. We never did, or never will, convince many Americans that we belong to the Royal Air Force (rather a smug title if you think about it). *'Say, you mean the Royal CANADIAN Air Force?'* 'No, the *Royal Air Force.'* Puzzled look, *'But what country's that? Australia?* It was often easier to anticipate all this and say we were the *'Royal British Air Force.'*! I found the USA of those days only grew slowly on me. First reactions were that there was much of which to be contemptuous. The brashness, the sameness, the lack of tradition. But in time the brashness became friendliness, the sameness meant a quality and cleanliness that you could rely on. And the lack of long standing heritage meant that they valued what they had.

An enduring impression is the earnest American. A group of us were on a tour of the Boulder Dam. The guide was rattling off facts on quantities, height, volumes, depths and the like. During a slight pause, our Flight Engineer turns to our party and says, *'I hope you're taking this all in, there are questions afterwards!'*

Regulations and notices proliferate. In one of my USAF rooms, somewhere, was a notice:

'In accordance with Air Force Order 103-B-10J/1, Section 10D, Part 9, Sub-section 4B-10, division 7A, paragraph 79, Smoking in Bed is STRICTLY Forbidden'—to which a wit had added:

'Sleeping in the ash trays is also not allowed.'

In an Officers' Club Bar I saw a placard, one day, in the familiar style, which I idly read:

NOTICE AS REQUIRED BY AIR FORCE ORDER 79/21 – D – 71A

Office of Civilian Defense
Washington D.C.

INSTRUCTIONS TO PATRONS ON PREMISES
IN CASE OF NUCLEAR BOMB ATTACK

UPON THE FIRST WARNING

1. Stay clear of all windows.

2. Keep hands free of glasses, bottles, cigarettes etc.

3. Stand away from bar, tables, orchestra equipment and furniture.

4. Loosen necktie, unbutton coat and other restrictive clothing.

5. Remove glasses, empty pockets of all sharp objects such as pens, pencils etc.

6. Immediately upon seeing the brilliant flash of the nuclear explosion, bend over and place your head firmly between your legs.

7. Then kiss your ass goodbye.

Less vulgar was the addition to the notice on the Jukebox. 'Unless the interference with this machine's volume control ceases then it will be removed.'—the postscript ... 'Promises, promises!'

Life in the United States Air Force seemed a lot more serious than ours. Earnest young men struggled for promotion. If they did not make it, then they left the service. Those that did make it became even more serious with their intent to retain and further advance their promotion. One commander suffered a severe blow to his ambitions when his base was subject, in his absence, to a surprise inspection by his Major General. His verdict: 'Colonel, you are dismissed.' The Colonel pleaded, 'But Sir, this is unfair, I was on leave at the time.' 'You were unlucky,' replied the MG, 'And I can't afford to have unlucky commanders!'

With the Boscombe Down Britannia we used to spend a lot of time at Homestead AFB in Florida. This was in support of Maritime Nimrod trials at the Bahamas underwater range at Andros Island. It was a regular commitment for 'B' Squadron, the Multi-Engine Test Squadron, so much so that when a couple of AEOps found themselves with a spare bottle of duty free, they buried it in the motel garden—and recovered it the next year! Rather inappropriately the motel was in the Howard Johnson chain—the teetotal combine!

Andros Island provided some excitement for us Boscombe Britannia people. We were required to land and take off on its crushed coral runway, which was just 4000 feet long. The Britannia was the largest aircraft that had used this runway.

Runways provide quite a topic for tales in the crewroom. A couple of young inexperienced pilots were struggling, in bad visibility, to find the airfield. Suddenly ahead the concrete appeared; touchdown right on the 'button' but then it was brakes hard on as the end rapidly appeared out of the gloom—they just stopped. *'Phew!'* said one, *'that runway was short!'* *'Yeah,'* said the other, looking left and right, *'but wide though!'* They had landed across it!'

Many large airports have parallel runways, designated 'Left' and 'Right'. A particularly cool US airline captain was running short of fuel, a situation he had to declare in order to secure a priority landing. Air Traffic became anxious about his fuel remaining and where he would divert if he was unable to land in the poor weather that prevailed. *'Elf Air Nina-Zero you are cleared to land, Runway 27 Left—what is your diversion?'* Back came the laconic reply, *'27 Right?'*

Air Traffic can be a measure of a country's state of civilization. In its emerging days the service is likely to be manned by 'ex-pats'; but as independence is secured so is a take-over of the controlling services. It was early days for one embryonic nation and one of the locals was given full rein in the control tower. An aircraft is on finals to land, *Ult Air Five-Four is three miles final, gear checked to land.'* *'Ult Air Fave Fure—cleared to land—roger.'* There is a pause with aircraft nearing the runway, which now gives the pilot the opportunity of realising that there is another aircraft sitting on the end, waiting to take-off. *'Ult Air Five Four is overshooting—you clown—there was an aircraft on the runway.'* Back comes a mournful transmission, *'Oh dear—another of days as yesterday!'*

The overshoot might well have meant a message of apology over the PA system from the Captain to pacify the passengers. This form of communication can provide a 'banana skin'. One Britannia Captain fell foul of a sticking microphone switch. As the aircraft taxied in at some particuarly hot destination, the Captain did his bit on the PA *'hoping that you have had a comfortable flight and we wish you a safe journey to your final destinations. Good Day.'* A pause—and the ears in the passenger cabin prick up as through the air comes, *'Cor, what I could do with now is a cold drink and a hot woman!'* The female ALM leaps from her seat and rushes towards the flight deck to prevent any further 'messages'. One of the passengers leans into the aisle as she passes, *'You've forgotten the cold drink!'*

Some Captains can say too much, getting carried away by the sound of their own voices and the facility of a captive audience—and they can try to be too clever. It was top of descent time. A groan goes up from the passengers as through the loudspeakers comes a voice now only too

familiar to them—the Captain had given them the full treatment of ' ... *and we are flying at twenty thousand feet ... if you look out of the windows on your left you will see ...*' and so on, right through the trip. Now it was ' ... *and we have commenced our descent ... the weather is fine ... and the local time is, for the RAF boys on board 1800 hours, for the Navy that is 'Four Bells' and for the Army—Mickey Mouse is at the bottom of your watch and Donald Duck is at the top!*' A formal complaint was registered about this and Captain Tactless was subsequently 'interviewed'.

We did care a lot about our passengers. The sight of the 'crocodile' of them, viewed from the flight deck window, making their way from the passenger terminal, mostly women and children, could give one a chilling feeling of responsibility. Our Air Loadmasters and Air Stewards would do their best during the flight and there were invariably compliments and thanks at its end. This perhaps would be particularly from families who had endured long commercial flights which they could compare with our more relaxed atmosphere, with greater attention and much more room to move around.

But with this caring came leg pulling. Passengers could be easy meat for the practical joker. The latter would have an unfair advantage, being in a familiar environment in full possession of his faculties. It was often said that many passengers jettisonned most of their brains as they climbed the steps and inside the aircraft they could be in complete awe of all that was going on. Things were worse in the days of the Hastings. One of its passengers must have been in this numbed state of mind to fall for this one. The flight deck door opened and out backed the pilot, unrolling two lengths of tape as he goes. He furtively eyed his customers for one that looked gullible—the likely one is spotted, '*Please will you do me a favour, I'm dying to go to the loo.*' Puzzled look. '*The aircraft will probably fly by itself OK but can you hold these and if you feel the left wing go down pull this tape and if it's the right, pull this one.*' The passenger sat there white-knuckled whilst the Captain attended to his ablutions!

Perhaps there was not the awareness of autopilots in those far off days and yet these devices continued to be a useful tool for the hoaxer into our Britannia days. Before a flight an earnest young Army Lieutenant introduced himself to the crew and asked if he might visit the flight deck. He fed in the fact that he had started doing a little private flying. '*Come up*

front by all means,' says the Captain, *'In fact you can have a bit of a go at the controls.'* Soon after take-off the eager passenger is there. As the aircraft reaches cruising altitude the co-pilot vacates his seat and the Army person slides in. The Captain gives him a quick reminder of which way the control column has to be moved to do what, *'Oh, and you will find the controls very much heavier than in the light aircraft you have flown—off you go, you have control.'* The Army Lieutenant concentrates hard, detecting as soon as possible any deviation of the aircraft from straight and level flight. He does find the controls heavy—beads of perspiration appear on his forehead. This goes on for some time. When it had been decided that he had done enough, there was not the heart to tell him that the autopilot had been engaged the whole time!

That crew deserved to have the smile wiped from their faces by the autopilot then going unserviceable—when this did happen then it was a real hardship for the two pilots. One crew was stuck with this condition for a number of legs in the same aircraft. A fresh set of passengers are boarding. One young man, although in civilian clothes, clearly identified himself by his accoutrements as a fairly new RAF pilot. '*Here comes the autopilot*', choruses the crew.

Our autopilot had an amber light that would illuminate when the disengage button was pressed on the control column. This could be done undetected by the young lady sitting on the engineer's seat, between the two pilots, who had been introduced to the light as being capable of detecting 'True or False'. The questions asked I leave to your imagination. It was the age of the mini-skirt so it was quite possible that the same young lady had already been invited to look through the sextant, mounted in the flight deck roof. The adjustable platform to do this would have been put on its highest setting!

15
A Cold Spell

We had, with digression, been proceeding to parts of the world far removed from the 'Changi Slip'. One such place that would well qualify for that distinction would be the North Pole. The Britannias did have a regular Arctic commitment. This was to the Specialist Navigation Course for whom we flew, annually, two polar training flights. One of these was airborne for 13 hours and 15 minutes, possibly a record for the Britannia.

The intention of the flights was to allow the students to observe navigation equipment operating in the difficult environment of extreme latitudes. In the early days, the flights routed out of Lyneham to the North Pole and then to Thule AFB in Greenland. On this leg I was the co-pilot of the second crew, travelling as a passenger—a lowly position.

On the way to the Pole the news on the Thule weather was not good and it was decided at 87° North to forsake the Pole and turn for Thule. The subsequent approach there proved that the reports were not exaggerated—nothing was seen. The diversion airfield for Thule was Sondrestrom, holding the distinction of being particularly far away for an alternate airfield. On the overshoot a climb was made to 35,000 feet for the two hour flight. This really was on the limits of the fuel set aside for such a diversion and the height was essential to eke this out.

Communications were poor and an emergency had to be declared in order to convey the critical situation. It was a great relief as Sondrestrom hove into sight at the end of its fjord. The subsequent fuel checked revealed 3,000 lbs remaining—barely enough to wet the bottoms of the Britannia's several large fuel tanks.

There is a chilling sequel to this story. The next day we, the second crew, took off for the return flight to Lyneham. Climbing through 15,000 feet there was a bang and a rush of air. The pressurization had failed and the cabin altitude climbed rapidly. As we started an emergency descent the Air Quartermaster reported that the curtain over the entrance to the Gent's toilet was streaming rearwards. A valve in the toilet ground discharge mechanism had failed.

With fuel jettisonned, we landed back at Sondrestrom. Surprisingly we were airborne again a couple of hours later with a new valve made in the USAF workshops.

But why should this failure subsequent to the diversion the day before, produce a shudder? Reflect, as I have—the valve had not been touched since we left Lyneham. If it had failed on the previous pressurization—on the climb out of Thule—then disaster would have resulted. The aircraft would have been forced to climb to 35,000 feet in order that the diversion could be accomplished with the fuel available. The crew had oxygen but there was none for the 40-plus passengers. Man does not survive at 35,000 feet without oxygen for two hours!

Another venture of mine, into the Arctic Circle, was a flight to Churchill AFB on the Hudson Bay. It was cold—it was very cold. But there was insulation. A heated crew bus was waiting at the bottom of the steps ready to whisk us to our accommodation. This was linked, by corridors, to all the domestic facilities we required. And it was all heated, nay super-heated. In this environment you could forget about the cold outside until the morning, but the aircraft had endured the cold all night. The degree of this could be judged by the plastic bags that we used for our headsets. It was noticeable in the temperature ranges that we normally flew how the consistency of these changed from hard in cold to a limp softness in the tropics. Here, in the Churchill cold, they shattered! In the short time you spent outside, every intake of breath caused the nostril hairs to freeze.

Preparations for departure proceeded slowly in these conditions. There were two aircraft there and heaters were needed to allow each process of the pre-flight to proceed. We started up and taxied out first. There was always a last hurdle before a Britannia take-off. A protective device against engine distintegration caused by a runaway turbine could not be checked fully until full power was being applied. The throttles were advanced, the call came that the system checked out—'Limiters armed'—and we rolled down the runway, No problem here of sluggish-ness as our engines devoured that powerful cold air. We were airborne and away from that hostile environment. Our compatriots were not so lucky; their 'limiters' did not 'arm'. So back to dispersal they went—and the aircraft became colder and colder. As it sat there with attempts being made to cure the one fault, more faults developed. Hydraulic fluid started dripping from joints. That aircraft was at Churchill for over a week. A clear illustration that this converted airliner was never intended to operate in such an alien environment.

I had a laugh: flying in to Churchill had been my first 'route check' as a squadron co-pilot by an examiner who had not been particularly helpful in my training. He had transferred to the other aircraft for his next leg.

With all this aggravation from the cold, you might well ask why we had gone into such a place. I cannot remember but there must have been a reason; possibly it was to take equipment for cold weather trials— missiles? We often carried guided missiles, laid out, carefully, at intervals on the cargo floor. I often mused whether the heat-seeking type 'eyed' the Air Loadmaster as he carried a tray of hot drinks from the galley, up the aircraft, to the flight deck. There was a tale (apochryphal?) of the ALM, with such a load, who came on to the flight deck just before start-up with his papers to be signed by the Captain. This done, he waves a fist full of short rods with labels under the Captain's nose. '*I've got all the safety pins, skipper.*' Admittedly they were labelled, for their fighter aircraft application, 'REMOVE PINS BEFORE FLIGHT'! A particularly ancient Air

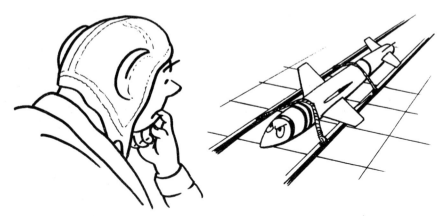

Loadmaster, hearing this story being retold by a new and youthful co-pilot, retaliates with the tale of . . .

. . . the Crewroom door swings closed. Your privileged stay to listen to the 'Tales' is over. The private brotherhood—with the occasional sister— is re-established. Events will create more stories to be retold and in with them will be mixed some of those we have been able to share. The folklore cycle continues.

Older people tend to think that 'things aren't like they used to be'. Older fliers definitely feel that the younger generation will never operate in the same atmosphere as they did. But I'm sure they are wrong. There will always be 'Tales from the Crewroom'.